Listening to the Animals

IN THE
WILD

EDITED BY PHYLLIS HOBE

A GUIDEPOSTS BOOK

ACKNOWLEDGMENTS

Every attempt has been made to credit the sources of copyrighted material used in this book. If any such acknowledgment has been inadvertently omitted or miscredited, receipt of such information would be appreciated.

All material that originally appeared in *Guideposts* magazine or *Daily Guideposts* is reprinted with permission. Copyright © 1982, 1986, 1987, 1992, 1995.

"The Voice in the Woods" and "Message From a Hawk" are from *Love, Miracles, and Animal Healing*, by Allen M. Schoen, D.V.M., and Pam Proctor. Copyright © 1995 by Allen M. Schoen, D.V.M., and Pam Proctor. Published by Simon & Schuster.

"The Bear and the Camper" and "The Field Hand" are from *Animal Angels*, a special Guideposts edition of *Peaceful Kingdom*, by Stephanie Laland. Copyright © 1997 by Stephanie Laland. Published by Conari Press.

"Lie Down With Lions," by David E. Petzal, is from *Field & Stream*, January 1998.

"Newborn," by Dr. Vaughan A. Langman, is from *Tall Blondes*, by Lynn Sherr. Copyright © 1997 by Lynn Sherr. Published by Andrews McMeel Publishing.

"It's a Girl!" is from *Daisy Rothschild*, by Betty Leslie-Melville. Copyright © 1987 by Betty Leslie-Melville. Published by Doubleday & Company, Inc.

"A Perfect Den" is from *The Hidden Life of Dogs*, by Elizabeth Marshall Thomas. Copyright © 1993 by Elizabeth Marshall Thomas. Published by Houghton Mifflin Company.

"Tiger!" by Stanley Breeden is from *National Geographic*, December 1984.

"A Moose for Jessica" is a condensation of the book, *A Moose for Jessica*, by Pat A. Wakefield with Larry Carrara. Copyright © 1987 by Pat A. Wakefield and Larry Carrara. Published by E. P. Dutton.

"Buffalo Games," as excerpted in *Chicken Soup for the Pet Lover's Soul* (by Jack Canfield, Mark Victor Hansen, Marty Becker, D.V.M., and Carol Kline), is from *Winterdance*, by Gary Paulsen.

"A Big, Ugly Baby" is from *Clem: The Story of a Raven*, by Jennifer Owings Dewey. Copyright © 1986 by Jennifer Owings Dewey. Published by Dodd, Mead & Company.

"The Hemlock Pair" and "Three Gray Whales" are from *Animals Who Have Won Our Hearts*, by Jean Craighead George. Copyright © 1994 by Jean Craighead George. Published by HarperCollins Publishers.

"Mama Robin" is from *Sweet Hope Waiting*, by Barbara Earl Thomas, and was reprinted in *Intimate Nature*, edited by Linda Hogan, Deena Metzger, and Brenda Peterson. "In the Presence of Dolphins," by Toni G. Frohoff, is from *Beyond Species* and was reprinted in *Intimate Nature*. Copyright © 1998 by Brenda Peterson, Deena Metzger, and Linda Hogan. Published by Fawcett Books, The Ballantine Publishing Group.

(continued on page 208)

Designed by SMS Typography
Illustrations by Ron Bucalo
Jacket designed by Dennis Arnold
Printed in the United States of America

Contents

In the Sky

CONTENTS   v

IN THE WATERS

BACKYARD NEIGHBORS

SHARING OUR EARTH

Introduction

In the Wild takes you on an adventure into parts of the world where many of us have never been. In these true stories you will meet animals—and some people—most of us rarely encounter.

Animals who live in the wild are very different from those who share our homes and lives. They have their own communities and traditions that go back to the beginning of time, and they would just as soon avoid human beings because they haven't always been treated well by them.

But things are changing. As more and more wild areas are becoming civilized, the animals we used to see only from a distance are now much closer to us. Our lives are beginning to overlap and, slowly, we are learning about each other. Perhaps the most important lesson for us is that we and the animals in the wild share God's creation, and it is time for us to become better acquainted.

The stories in ON THE LAND take us into woods and mountains, hills and valleys, and bring us up close to some of the animals who live there. Stephanie Laland tells us about a camper who was befriended by a large bear who traveled with him for a few days, sharing some of the fish he caught and resting with him by his campfire. David Petzal had quite a different experience when he slept outside his tent one night in lion country.

But Jock and Betty Melville had a much longer friendship with a young giraffe they were protecting from poachers. A little closer to home, we meet a moose that dares to come out of the shelter of the woods to be with a cow named Jessica.

IN THE SKY leads us up into the world of birds. We meet Clem, a baby raven rescued and loved by Jennifer Owings Dewey, who knows only too well that the bird will eventually leave. Fairly Chandler, on the other hand, finds comfort in discovering that sparrows not only leave but return. And if you aren't exactly enchanted by vultures, you may change your mind after you read "A Bell for Rajah," by John K. Terres.

Very few of us have the opportunity, or the skill, to get close to animals IN THE WATERS, so these stories fascinate us. Imagine yourself, like Toni G. Frohoff, making eye contact with dolphins while you're out for a swim. Or trying to free three whales trapped in ice off the coast of Alaska. Don C. Reed also keeps us in suspense as he approaches a shark that needs help.

Perhaps the most overlooked animals in the wild are our BACKYARD NEIGHBORS, the little, scurrying creatures we see around our houses, in parks, on city streets, and in almost every tree. Nathan Zimelman makes us cheer when he describes what happens to a woodsy city alleyway, a favorite hangout for wildlife, that was torn up and paved over but eventually restored by the forces of nature. Chris Ferris shares her satisfaction after freeing a fox from a snare. And Sue Monk Kidd gains some insight into her relationship with her teenaged son after watching a mother bird rebuild a broken nest again and again and again.

SHARING OUR EARTH is a flat-out realization that we and our wild creatures must respect and help each other. We go along with a team of animal rescuers to pull a wounded wood-

chuck out of danger on a busy highway. We watch veterinarians tend to a sick hawk and a porcupine in an animal
emergency room. We walk with Jane Goodall among a family
of chimpanzees and learn, from Elizabeth C. Reed, what it's
like to babysit a white tiger cub in your own home.

As we learn more about the animals we don't often see,
we can't help but feel a kinship with them. We need them in
our world and they need us in order to continue living here. We
are, after all, God's creatures and we share his world. The stories
in *In the Wild* teach us how to become each other's friends.

PHYLLIS HOBE

IN THE
WILD

On the Land

"*Make us, ourselves, to be true friends to the animals and so to share the blessings of the merciful.*"

ALBERT SCHWEITZER

Early one morning, while walking my dog along a country road, I looked across the fields toward the ridge where the sun was rising. There I saw two does and two fawns standing absolutely still, watching me. I stood still, too, because it was such a beautiful sight. After a few seconds they turned, their white tails flashing an alarm, and disappeared over the ridge.

I was grateful for the glimpse of them. They will never walk beside me as my dog does, but my world is a better place because they are in it.

The Voice in the Woods

ALLEN M. SCHOEN AND PAM PROCTOR

My career plans were at a crossroads during my last year at college. I was drawn to the traditional, "safe" path of medical school—a choice that I knew would please my parents. I had also worked one summer as a paramedical assistant with the Christian Medical Society in the Dominican Republic and Haiti, and felt a tug toward working with the sick in such impoverished areas. But my heart was leading me to become a veterinarian. I applied to school in both fields, and automatically assumed that getting into vet school would be considerably easier than making it into medical school. But in a strange turn of events, I was put on the waiting list at vet school—and was offered a scholarship to medical school.

Now I was more than a little confused about the path I should take. Should I seize the bird in the hand—medicine—and pursue a career working with people? Or should I take a risk, try again, and follow my original longing to become a veterinarian?

To find an answer, I did what I had always done as a child: when in doubt, I went back to nature. I jumped in the beat-up old Chevy I had been given for graduation and headed West. I had so little money that I didn't even have a tent. All I had was a sleeping bag and an old backpack with a knife, a flashlight, some fishing line, and a hook. I went from the Rockies to the Sierra Nevada to the Cascades, hiking alone along rugged trails that ended in desolate peaks where I would camp out under the stars. As I trekked along, playing hide-and-seek with marmots and black swallowtails and moose, I asked God to show me which path to take.

Then one day, out of nowhere, I seemed to hear a voice say, "I want you to become a veterinarian."

I didn't think it odd that God should speak to me directly. After all, I had been speaking to Him ever since my youthful musings in the apple tree in Queens. If God's temple is nature, as the ancient Jewish mystics of the Kabala had said, then it was only fitting that His voice should echo in the midst of His creation.

If I needed any confirmation of this revelation, I got it—in a dramatically symbolic stroke—on top of Mount Olympus, the highest peak in the Olympic Mountains in Washington State. With very little food in my pack, I had foolishly headed up the mountain's main slope. I expected that the trek would take only two days, but as two days stretched into three, I was beginning to get worried.

I had no choice but to do what Native Americans had done and live off the land. Luckily, I had taken a course in biosurvival in college. So I threw myself on the mercy of nature and foraged for wild carrots, onions, and dandelions along the trail. With my fishing line and hook, I caught a couple of fish in a mountain lake, grilled them on a stick over the fire, and settled down for an uneasy night's sleep.

About 2 A.M., I was suddenly awakened by the sound of crashing in the bushes. I grabbed my flashlight and tiptoed over to the source of the noise. As quietly as I could, I parted the bushes and beamed the flashlight into the blackness. There, just a few feet away, a struggle to the death was taking place between a ferret and a snake. The ferret held the snake tight between its teeth and was flipping it back and forth mercilessly. A few moments later, the snake grew limp. The ferret, no longer absorbed by the contest, turned his head toward the light and stared in my direction.

My body tingled with excitement. Here was nature in the raw—a primal environment in which I was just another inhabitant. In the wild, I realized the ferret and I were not really so different. Each of us was living from minute to minute, using our skill and resourcefulness to survive. But even more, I had a sense that somehow the ferret and I were interconnected. Perhaps he had actually saved me from danger by killing the snake. I'll never know. All I know is that as I watched the ferret slink off into the night, dragging the snake along with him, I no longer felt alone.

A few days later on the shores of Glacier Lake in Montana, I found another unexpected companion. I had been fishing for about an hour with no luck when suddenly I felt a tug at my line. And just as I was about to reel in what I hoped was my evening meal, a playful otter popped out of the water. His little face seemed to be grinning at some secret joke—until I realized that the joke was on me.

He dove back into the water and a few seconds later emerged triumphantly with a fish in his mouth. Then as if to mock me, he waved the fish back and forth at me, and dove back under again.

"Hey," I called out. "That's *my* fish!"

Otters are notorious clowns, and this one was enticing me into a game. For the next hour or so, we engaged in a "conversation," as I continued to wait for a catch and he playfully bobbed and circled nearby. The sun was beginning to drop behind the mountain when at long last I made my first catch of the day.

"I got one!" I shouted, holding it up for my friend to admire.

"Eeek! Eeek!" he barked in approval. Then, with our game at a draw, he cocked his head, dove into the water, and swam away.

It didn't take long for me to start missing him. Somehow, we had understood each other, this otter and I. In our brief time together, communicating through gestures and sounds, we had developed the beginnings of a friendship. I had been comforted by his presence and buoyed by his spirited high jinks; he had clearly relished my companionship—especially the chance to perform for an audience.

As I made my way back to civilization, I realized that my wilderness trek had been a prelude to the much larger journey that lay ahead of me. Through the ferret that had protected me and the otter that had played with me, I began to understand that, somehow, nature itself was placing a seal of approval on my decision to devote my life in the service of animals. By the time I arrived home, I was firmly committed to putting all my energies into becoming an animal doctor.

from LOVE, MIRACLES, AND ANIMAL HEALING

The Bear and the Camper

STEPHANIE LALAND

$\mathcal{R}$obert Franklin Leslie put up his lean-to and prepared to camp deep in the Canadian woods. The outdoorsman had spent thirty years hiking through the most isolated reaches of North America. When he climbed down to a nearby stream, he found himself with most unexpected company.

Thirty yards away stood a giant black bear. Robert knew he dare not make any fast movements. He also knew that the bear could kill him if he wanted to. Adventurer that he was, though, Robert decided to proceed calmly down to the stream and go fishing.

The bear followed.

Robert made slow, careful movements as he baited his hook and started to fish. The bear, who shared his interest in fishing, settled down just five feet away and watched attentively. Then Robert caught his first fish—fourteen inches—and tossed it to the bear.

The bear gulped it down and waited appreciatively until Robert caught another, which also went down the bear's gullet. And another. Robert fished and fed his catch to the bear until nightfall. Then he decided to head back to camp and cook up a couple of fish he had caught for himself.

The bear followed. Robert named him Bosco and spoke softly to him.

Robert made a campfire, ate his fish, and settled down to sleep in his sleeping bag. Bosco decided to settle down with his new fish-catching friend. Man and bear stretched out together under a tarp and enjoyed their quiet companionship. The smell of wet, furry, fish-sated bear filled Robert's nostrils. He decided it was rather a good smell.

Bosco got up in the night and attempted to scratch the lower part of his back, just above his tail—a difficult place to reach. He came to Robert, obviously asking for help. Inspecting the itchy spot carefully, Robert saw that it was full of fat ticks that were irritating the bear's flesh. The first tick he pulled out caused Bosco to roar so loudly it jolted the forest. For a moment, Robert thought the bear would kill him, but then Bosco seemed satisfied when he saw Robert pitch the tick into the flames. Extracting each tick from the inflamed flesh, Robert held it up for the bear to sniff and then cast it into the fire.

As they returned to sleep, Bosco was careful not to put the full 500 pounds of his weight against Robert. The bear's cold nose woke Robert up several times as he came and went during the night. The next morning, to Robert's extreme delight, Bosco chose to follow him as he hiked to the next destination.

Robert and Bosco got to know each other very well. They romped and wrestled. If Bosco's play became too rough, Robert had only to roll over and play dead to find Bosco whimpering and licking his face.

Robert chopped open a tree full of honeybees for Bosco,

scratched him when asked, and fished for him when the bear desired. It was all a bear could hope for.

Robert studied Bosco's movements and vocabulary. Bosco would sometimes pick the man up in a heartfelt embrace that gave true meaning to the term "bear hug," and he would lick Robert's face.

Perhaps the best times of all were at night by the campfire, when Bosco would stare deeply into the man's eyes and commune as if the two were Man and Nature itself delving deep into one another. Bosco enjoyed this profound contemplation and, at the end of it, would often put a gargantuan paw upon the man's shoulder as if some meaningful point about the nature of life had been reached.

One day Bosco gave a signal to Robert not to move as they hiked through the woods. Suddenly they were surrounded by four bears. These bears were younger than Bosco, only two-year-olds, whereas Bosco was full-grown. He beat back each one in turn.

That night at camp, Bosco wanted to spend extra time gazing into Robert's eyes, although Robert didn't yet understand the reason for this. Perhaps the encounter earlier that day had reminded Bosco more fully that he was a bear, not a man. The next day, as they were hiking, Bosco ambled off in another direction. Robert didn't call to him. The bear didn't look back. Robert wrote, "He left behind a relationship I shall treasure."

from ANIMAL ANGELS

Lie Down With Lions

DAVID E. PETZAL

$\mathcal{S}$noring is a given in all hunting camps. No matter where on earth you bunk, someone is going to have a throat full of phlegm and adenoids the size of volleyballs. It was in a tent camp in Africa, however, where snoring nearly turned me into a lion snack.

The camp was called *Phuduhudu* (Bakwena for steenbok) and was pitched in prime lion country near a village called Kang, in Botswana's Kalahari Desert. Unlike most camps in lion country, which are fairly elaborate, ours was simply a collection of canvas tents and was not surrounded by a *boma*, or thornbush wall, to keep the kitties out.

There were three of us in one tent. One slept quietly, but the other was a snorer of operatic caliber. It was a terrible, blubbering snore that began at ear-shattering levels and grew louder from there. There was a metallic element to it that sounded like a big engine tearing itself apart. . . .

I woke up my noisy friend repeatedly, and after apologizing profusely, he'd fall right back to sleep and start in all over again. Finally, I'd had enough, and dragged my cot out of the tent and into the center of camp. Looking up at the constellations of the southern hemisphere, I congratulated myself on being a clever and resourceful fellow.

At dawn, I rolled out of the cot and looked down at the pink sand. There were the pugmarks of a very large lion who had strolled into camp, walked right up to me, taken a sniff, and decided that I was not as toothsome as a hartebeest.

I may be silly, but I ain't stupid. I took my cot back in the tent. There are, after all, worse things than a little snoring.

from FIELD & STREAM

Newborn

DR. VAUGHAN A. LANGMAN

*I*mmediately after birth, the giraffe cow moves her calf a short distance to an area of safety. Here the calf is completely isolated from all other giraffes for a period which may last as long as a month. During this time, the calf stays in the area, lying down and moving very little. The cow returns two to three times a day to allow the calf to nurse. She may go up to 15 miles away from the hidden calf for water or food. The calf waits for her to return. . . .

Over an extended period they hide their young in groups and provide "baby-sitting" services.

During the early morning, the giraffe cows with their calves will move to special areas that are used repeatedly by nursery herds. They all eat together for a while, and then the cows leave one by one. Soon only the calves remain; they lie down and nibble trees very near to where they were left. Two or three times during the day each cow returns to the nursery group and lets her calf suckle. The cows will then leave again, but at the end of the day return and stay with their calves to protect them during the night.

At night the nursery herd maintains one or two giraffes as watchmen to ensure that lions cannot approach unnoticed. They change watch regularly so that no giraffe is on duty all night. This is accomplished without a sound and without any apparent plan. . . .

Next morning all of the giraffes travel to an area similar to one where the calves were left the day before; and just as before, the cows begin to leave their calves and travel to feeding areas. However, this time not all the giraffe cows leave; one mother remains behind with all the other calves. Yesterday's hidden group of calves becomes a calf pool with one mother as the baby-sitter. How that giraffe cow becomes sitter for the day is not clear. At first glance it seems so planned that you think each cow takes turns. It is more likely that the baby-sitting cow feels no urge to drink or seek out special feeding areas and simply stays behind because she lacks a motive for leaving.

from TALL BLONDES

"It's a Girl!"

BETTY LESLIE-MELVILLE

I met my husband, Jock, in Kenya. We were married there and bought a big, old stone house, on the outskirts of Nairobi, that we loved. We loved looking at Mount Kilimanjaro, 110 miles away, and walking in the forest. But best of all was the surprise we got when we saw three wild Maasi giraffe on our property and realized they lived there, too. It was a thrilling sight to see the tallest animals in the world standing in front of the tallest mountain in Africa. We would sit in our living room and watch them strolling down the driveway, munching the trees they fancied, destroying our shrubs, and stomping the flowers along the way. We named them Tom, Dick, and Harry.

One day a friend came to see us and said he had the only 130 Rothschild giraffe left in the world living on his ranch, and that they were being poached. He asked us, "Would you take just one? You'd be helping to save an endangered species. At least there would be one Rothschild *twiga* [Swahili for 'giraffe'] left."

"If we got a baby giraffe," I said enthusiastically to Jock, "it would live outside and just eat the trees, and we wouldn't have to do anything. . . . " Ha, little did I know.

"But how do we get one?" Jock asked.

"Baby giraffe and sea lions are the two animals that can't

take tranquilizers," our friend told us, "but I know a man who knows how to capture a baby giraffe from his horse. His name is Rutherfurd, and his horse's name is Douglas."

So Rutherfurd came to see us and promised to try to rope a baby giraffe for us. "Then we'll put it in a stable up there and give it a little milk for a few days. After that, we'll bring it to Nairobi." He didn't mention how dangerous the capture might be. Nor did he tell us that if he was successful at getting one, we would have to give it a bottle of milk four times a day for a year.

So, the following week, we merrily drove the 225 miles north to the ranch for the big event.

Early the next morning, Rutherfurd introduced us to Douglas, the only horse in the world able to attempt this hazardous undertaking. By nature, horses are terrified of giraffe. It had taken Rutherfurd three years to train Douglas to go into a herd. As if that were not bad enough, the land where the Rothschild giraffe live is dangerous because it is pocked with ant-bear holes two feet wide and three feet deep, hidden in the long grass. The nocturnal ant bears, or aardvarks, dig these enormous holes in a matter of minutes while searching for termites, and whether they find their food or not, the holes remain for years afterward, camouflaged by grass. It is impossible to drive a vehicle over the land, and no one in his right mind would ride a horse over it—no one but Rutherfurd, that is. And no one but Rutherfurd would ride Douglas, who is also said to be crazy.

Watching a large herd through his binoculars, Rutherfurd found a giraffe to try for. He kicked Douglas, and they were off like kamikaze pilots. Douglas concentrated on the ground, not having any idea where he was going, and Rutherfurd concentrated on the herd like a guided missile beamed into its target aircraft. To protect their babies, giraffe get them out front, as far away from the danger as possible, so Rutherfurd had to bore through the entire herd. The giraffe were running at a fantastic rate, flying hooves striking out at him, just missing him over and over again. He looked like a scurrying ant alongside the speeding giants. He looked as if he were drowning in giraffe. Some of the giraffe stumbled into ant-bear holes, turned somersaults, and rolled back on their feet again.

There was so much dust and confusion that for a moment we couldn't see Rutherfurd. But suddenly we saw him emerge in front of the herd, galloping after a baby. Riveted, watching through binoculars, we then saw him, still at full gallop, come alongside the little giraffe, reach out and throw his arm around its neck, then leap off Douglas and wrestle the baby to the ground. If Rutherfurd won the match, we'd have a giraffe; if the giraffe won, we'd have a funeral.

We picked our way through low bushes and grass so high we were unable to see, but soon we could just see Rutherfurd's head—and something else

Rutherfurd called, "It's a girl!"

And there she lay in the short marshy grass, her feet tied by a rope, with Rutherfurd struggling to hold her neck upright. (A giraffe's head must be kept up because if the animal lies prone or its head goes down, it can die in a matter of minutes from undigested food blocking its windpipe.)

We had picked out names in advance, so we went up and introduced ourselves to Daisy Rothschild, telling her we were her new parents. For us it was love at first sight, but she hated us. Her enormous eyes glared at us in fright, and those long, long eyelashes made her look like a very angry Daisy indeed.

We touched her—she was so soft and silky. I kissed her nose, I patted her head, I stroked her mane, which was a golden brown. Her little horns were tufted—they looked like two black paintbrushes sticking up out of her head. Three spots shaped just like butterflies ran down her beige neck in a row. She was so beautiful.

Rutherfurd slipped a rope over her head, untied her feet, and let her stand. That was when the fight began. I spoke to her softly and told her we loved her; she kicked us. Her front legs flew out at us at a terrible speed with a forward and downward punch, her neck was arched—she looked like a sea horse. We walked her, fighting all the way, to our minibus. Have you ever tried to get an angry giraffe into a minibus? Somehow we finally managed to shove her in and drove through the pocked land to the stable.

We dragged Daisy, still kicking wildly, out of the bus and into the stable, which we had padded with straw. After trying unsuccessfully to escape, she just stood there staring at us, obviously disturbed. Rutherfurd said we should leave her alone for a few hours while she got used to her surroundings. That evening we peeped in and found her just standing there motionless and looking miserable.

The next morning, we raced to the stables to find her standing in the same place. Rutherfurd said she would have to drink by the following morning or she would die of dehydration. All day, we sat taking turns holding out the pan of milk and talking to her. Of course, she had never seen a pan before and had no idea what it was. She wanted nothing to do with it and would not drink. As the day wore on, she looked even more unhappy.

We were so worried.

At dawn, we raced to her to find her so weak she was unable to stand. I started to cry, and Daisy actually had a tear in her eye, too. I could imagine her asking, "Why can't I run in the sunshine and sleep near my mother and drink her good milk? Where is she? Who are all these strange creatures who do not look like giraffe at all?" Yet I knew if we hadn't captured her, she would be dead within a year.

Forty-nine hours passed, and I feared she was going to die right then. But suddenly, for no apparent reason, she got to her feet, walked to the bowl of milk that Jock was holding, and put her face into it and drank! And drank! She seemed so surprised it was milk. She licked her mouth and nose, then looked at Jock, bent down, and kissed him—and from that minute on, Jock was her "mother"! Then she investigated our hands and put her head close to ours and sniffed us. We spoke softly to her all the time, but didn't try to touch her. A few hours later, we gave her some more milk. She sucked at it and sort of inhaled it, like some berserk vacuum cleaner. It would be all over her face and up her nostrils, but she'd just stick out her long, purple tongue and poke it up her nose. Then she'd drink some more, and, spluttering, she'd spray us thoroughly. Since the milk had lots of cod liver oil in it, in no time Jock and I smelled terrible.

The next morning, when we walked toward her stable, she had her leg out the top half of the door trying to get to her "mother," Jock, for more milk. Afterward she let us stroke her face and ears. She felt as soft as velvet.

We picked her some thorn tree branches that had yellow flowers blooming on them. She recognized them as her favorite food and seemed delighted as she nibbled away.

Watching your baby giraffe eating yellow flowers is like watching a real live birthday card.

Veterinarians and scientists had warned us of the difficulties we would have raising a giraffe. Although other people in Kenya had tried, none had been successful. A doctor of zoology, who had raised many wild animals, but not giraffe, told us the most important thing is love. He told us about a baby steenbok, a species of antelope extremely difficult to rear, that he had seen in a mechanic's garage hopping about the spare parts and rusty wrecks of cars. The African had found the little thing abandoned and fed it and took it with him everywhere. Asked what he fed it, the mechanic told him whatever he had to eat himself—sometimes a doughnut, a sandwich, sometimes some soup served in an old hubcap. It was then that the doctor, who had tried and tried unsuccessfully to raise a steenbok with vitamins and calcium and sophisticated drugs, suddenly realized that wild animals need love as much as food if they are to survive. He was adamant as he told us, "They must relate to one person, they must be loved by that person. Then they will imprint and live." (Imprinting is when an animal feels attached, or bonded, to another.)

Already Jock was Daisy's "mother," so we had hope.

The next morning, with the help of about six other men, we got Daisy sitting in the minibus for her journey to Nairobi.

At one point, Jock drove into a gas station. You can imagine the surprise on the attendant's face when he saw a giraffe in the minibus. He didn't have enough money to go to game parks, so he had never seen a giraffe before, and he thanked us for bringing her.

from DAISY ROTHSCHILD

A Perfect Den

ELIZABETH MARSHALL THOMAS

The hill had everything a wolf could want in a den site. Located about halfway between the summer grounds and winter grounds of a herd of caribou, the den was always within a few days' travel of good hunting. Better yet, in spring, when the pups were born and their mother stayed in the den to feed and warm them, the caribou, accompanied by fawns, were passing right by the hill on their way to their summer pasture. And in the fall, when the wolf pups were gangling adolescents with ravenous appetites, when they needed more food than ever before but couldn't yet help with the hunting, the caribou, fattened up for winter, were migrating right past the den again, going back to their calving grounds. Yet the hunting opportunities were not the only advantages of the hill. Seemingly the deposit of a glacier, its soil was sandy enough to dig but also firm enough to hold a shape, so the wolves could dig a den that would not collapse on them.

The hill was also an excellent lookout. In the center of a vast basin ringed by higher hills, it commanded a 360-degree view for many miles in all directions, and was bordered on the south side by a stream. The latter was particularly important, not only because denning wolves need water to drink yet cannot provision one another with water as they can with food, but also because the stream served as a fence. For their own safety, the seven pups were supposed to stay at the den, but there they would get lonely and would inevitably try to follow a departing adult. Naturally, the adults couldn't let this happen—the pups would slow them down and spoil their hunting—so they would leave by heading south, at least to start with, and would jump over the stream, which was so wide and so deep that the pups couldn't follow. And the water was so cold they wouldn't try to swim. Instead, they would stand on the bank, forlorn and crying, watching the adults, who were obviously torn between going and staying, as they reluctantly trotted away.

Thus, the question of why that particular hill had been chosen as a den site was easy to answer. Any wolf would want such a place. Furthermore, because few places in the world are so perfect, most wolves must make do with much less. Who, therefore, were the wolves who lived there, and why were they, and not some other wolves, the occupants? Wolves are well known to be territorial, which is to say that they lay claim to certain areas, which they defend as best they can from other wolves. Whatever wolves owned the den site wouldn't willingly share it with strange wolves. This alone would tend to keep a den site in a family, all the more so because wolves, like most birds and many other mammals, apparently prefer ancestral nesting places. But were the current occupants of the den descendants of the first settlers? Could a den have been occupied by the same family for several thousand years? Although theoretically anything is possible, such long tenure would be unlikely. Probably the excellent site changed hands from time to time. I came to see it as resembling a medieval fort, a castle, remote and isolated, with a little band of occupants, probably an extended family, who spent most of their days simply putting food on the table yet who stood ready to repel invaders and whose ownership could be traced back in time, even a long time, to a heroic ancestor who had built the castle or had wrested it from its previous occupants. Ownership had been handed from parent to child; the primogeniture of human beings is, after all, little more than favoring the dominant child. The more I thought about it, the more the ancient landed gentry of Europe came to seem like wolves, with one pair, the dominant male and female, owning a territory and the castles upon it and hunting the deer for miles around. Dominance and ownership were surely very closely tied.

This, obviously, is still true of wolves. For them, ownership of a den is crucial, since without a sheltering den a pack disintegrates. Adult wolves don't need dens; adults can withstand terrible exposure. But their infants cannot. Like human infants, wolf pups can barely keep themselves warm, let alone survive outdoors in an Arctic winter. Furthermore, since wolves must be almost full-grown to have any hope of surviving the first winter, which is the greatest killer of young wolves, they must be born as early in the year as possible so they have time to grow. To this end, wolves mate in February and bear their pups in March, long before the snow melts. Dens cannot be dug in the frozen earth, so a pair of wolves without a den will surely lose their pups to the weather. And in any group of wolves, no matter who is pregnant, the dominant female gets to give birth inside the den. Thus ownership and dominance are life itself to wolves. . . .

As for the wolves, around their ancient homestead lay a vast and empty tundra where, because the Arctic plants were small and ground-hugging, nothing resisted the wind. The wind would push the clouds or turn the wolves' fur but make no sound. In this lonely silence, under the radiant Arctic sun, the five adult wolves assumed their responsibilities with competence and skill, so seasoned by hard work and so accustomed to one another that they interacted rarely, if at all. There were no dominance displays among these lonely toilers— in the way of all close families, they well knew who was who without reminding one another. And anyway, like a hard-working farm family or a lonely band of hunter-gatherers, the wolves had little time for anything but winning their livelihood from an unforgiving world.

Traveling singly or in pairs, four of them at any given time would almost always be hunting far away, while the fifth stayed at the den to babysit, often so tired that he or she would spend the entire time sleeping high on a ledge, out of reach of the pestering youngsters. For a while the pups would try to reach the babysitter, but eventually they would give up, fall silent, realize that everyone had gone and that the sitter wouldn't play with them, wait a few minutes longer, as if hoping they'd been mistaken, but at last creep inside the den. Yet not to forget about the outside world—the moment a hunter returned, bringing food, the pups would rush out and mob him. . . .

It became my impression that as boring as so provincial and mundane a life might seem to modern urban people, the wolves liked it. The orderly life, the daily routine, and the silent tundra in its annual gyre around the sun may have offered welcome predictability to those caribou hunters, each of whom was obliged, every few days, to travel a great distance alone, first to search for a likely victim, then to close in on it, then, if possible, to attack it, and finally to bring it down. An adult Baffin wolf is less than half the size of an adult Baffin caribou, and caribou are virtually the only large prey on the island. But they are not easy prey, especially since both sexes have antlers, and especially not for wolves, who have no claws with which to seize them, let alone guns, spears, or arrows with which to kill them from afar.

from THE HIDDEN LIFE OF DOGS

Tiger!

STANLEY BREEDEN

We set off at sunrise on this winter morning in central India, once again riding Pawan Mala, an old and venerable elephant. Out on the meadows the swamp deer stags are rutting. A tiger roars in the distance, a good omen.

Mahavir, the mahout, steers the elephant toward the tiger's stirring sound. We soon find fresh tiger footprints along a sandy ravine, or nullah—the broad strong pugs of a male. They lead us into dense forest.

We are on the right track; we can smell where the tiger has sprayed a bush to mark his territory. Belinda, my wife, sees the tiger first, an awesome vision in fiery orange and black stripes gliding through the green bamboo tracery. Ignoring us, he walks on and on. We are alongside him now, about 30 feet distant. Once or twice he glances at us and snarls, pale yellow-green eyes burning.

Suddenly the tiger stops in his tracks. He sees a herd of spotted deer browsing on bamboo at the edge of a small clearing. He makes not a motion—no tail twitch, no ear movement, not even a whisker quivers. He is frozen in the partial cover of a small patch of grass. As long as he is motionless, the deer cannot see him, even at 30 or 40 feet. There is no breeze, so they cannot scent him.

Slowly the tiger lies down. For half an hour or more he watches the deer. Then, carefully placing one foot in front of the other so as not to make a sound in the dry leaf litter, he insinuates himself from bush to bush. Closer and closer he moves. It seems our hearts have stopped beating.

Though grazing quietly, the deer are alert. Some does are especially watchful. One sniffs the air; there must be a faint tiger scent, for the doe stamps a forefoot, a sign of mild alarm. The others look up.

The tiger is rigid in a crouch, powerful hind feet gathered under him. The doe stamps her front foot again, raises her tail, gives her bell-like alarm call. The tiger bursts from cover, tail erect, ears forward. In unbelievably fast bounds he rushes the deer. They scatter. . . .

He misses, snarls, and utters a series of moaning roars. Then he rests, lying in a pool of sunlight. We go closer, to be greeted with a snarl and a low, rumbling growl. Never before or since have we seen a tiger with such a bad disposition. We name the tigers we study. This one is Snarl.

from NATIONAL GEOGRAPHIC

The Mystery of the Moose

ERIC FELLMAN

*D*uring last summer's canoe trip, I took some time to slip away by myself and try a new fishing lure. The evening drifted into that wonderful quietness when the daytime creatures grow silent and the nighttime creatures have not yet awakened. There was only the barest of ripples on the surface of the water as my canoe glided into a secluded bay.

Just before I tossed the first cast, my eye caught some movement up against the boulders along the far shore. An enormous bull moose was standing knee deep in the lake, feeding on the water grass. I sat quietly watching for several minutes while my canoe drifted to within a few yards of the moose. His antlers must have measured five feet across. *How does he ever move through the dense forest?* I wondered. I knew that he would stay near the lake in spring and summer, but for fall and winter would have to move into the forest to find shelter from the winter storms.

So intrigued was I with this question that I did some research when I got home, and found the answer for the moose. You see, when fall comes, the moose sheds his antlers and is able to move freely through the trees.

This discovery also gave me an answer for myself, as I looked at the forest of decisions that I faced in my work. I saw that it was my fears and doubts that were keeping me from moving forward. By listing the pros and cons of each decision, I have been able to shed my fears and move decisively through the forest into the future.

A Moose for Jessica

PAT A. WAKEFIELD AND LARRY CARRARA

It began with Ike, the dog, barking.

Larry Carrara and his wife, Lila, were having breakfast early that Saturday morning when Ike set up a fearful racket outdoors. The cows joined in, bellowing.

"What on earth is going on?" asked Lila.

Larry excused himself and went to see.

He stood on the front porch and gazed out at the late October countryside. His farm, called Carrara's Mountain, sits high in the hills of Shrewsbury, Vermont. The main road cuts through his property, only fifteen feet from the old colonial farmhouse.

Across the road, three of his cows were grazing in a pasture bordering twenty or so acres of heavily wooded land. Things looked all right there. He glanced at the cattle in the pasture next to his house. Nothing strange there, either. Larry went back inside.

The bellowing and barking resumed, however, so he got up again. Now the cows across the road were mooing loudly, staring into the woods. Larry scanned the stand of trees at the far side of the pasture. This time he saw something—over in the low bushes at the woods' edge. "What the . . . ? The branches are rotating like radar antennas," he said to himself.

A few seconds later, it dawned on him. Antlers.

At first he thought a deer was in the bushes. But when the antlers emerged and Larry saw the size of the body that followed, he knew differently. He shouted to Lila, "Quick! Come outside! You'll never believe it. There's a moose on our property. Hurry up before he runs away!"

Lila had never seen a moose. Most people have never seen a moose—even people who live in the mountains of Vermont. Moose are wild and solitary, and usually stay deep in the woods. So Lila was very excited as she ran to join Larry.

Larry had crossed the road for a closer look. The moose's shape and coloring provided effective camouflage. Its slender, silvery legs blended in with the tree trunks and brush, and its brownish black body faded into the dark shadows behind the trees. Its forked antlers could easily be mistaken for branches.

Now Larry was not more than twenty feet from a moose, and he was amazed at its size. He guessed it must be at least six feet tall from ground to shoulders, with antlers towering like a crown two feet above its huge head.

Lila crept up beside Larry, and they edged closer to the fence between the cow pasture and the woods. The moose didn't seem to notice them. It kept browsing on the branches of the balsam tree—pulling twigs into its mouth with its strong, fleshy upper lip; stripping the bark with its teeth; collecting the pieces with its lips; swallowing rapidly while still chewing.

As the moose stretched its neck to reach the higher branches, Lila whispered, "He's so big. He's the most beautiful thing I've ever seen in Shrewsbury, really. Look how he carries his antlers so proud."

The antlers were magnificent. They looked like huge, long-fingered hands, turned palms up. When the moose glanced toward Larry and Lila, Larry noticed the left one had a prong, or "finger," that curved down instead of up. He thought it might have been injured while the antler was still soft and forming.

By now Ike had stopped barking, and the cows were grazing peacefully. The moose continued to browse, periodically glancing toward the cows. If they saw him, they seemed undisturbed.

Twice while they watched, the moose lay down for about half an hour to chew his cud. Then he got up and browsed again. Finally, late in the afternoon, he stopped browsing, walked back along the fence, and disappeared into the woods.

Soon he reappeared on the other side of the fence, walking down the old logging road that led from the woods into the pasture where the three cows were grazing.

As the moose entered the pasture, one cow and a yearling calf took off like a shot and jumped the electric wire fence. The third cow, Jessica, a pudgy brown and white Hereford with a freckled nose, stood her ground and kept a wary eye on the unlikely visitor.

The moose walked around Jessica in tighter and tighter circles. Whenever he came within a few feet of her, she would demurely step away.

As the sun began to set, Larry and Lila realized they had been watching the moose all day. As they looked back into the pasture, the silhouettes of the moose and Jessica stood out against the dusky light.

That night, as Lila and Larry went to bed, they talked about how lucky they felt. They could hardly believe that the moose had stayed all day. They were sure he would be gone by morning.

When Larry woke up, the first thing he did was look out the window. He could see Jessica standing by a small shed in the pasture across the road, but he didn't see the moose.

He got dressed and went outside to do his chores, which included bringing Jessica some grain in a pail. When she finished eating, he picked up the pail and rounded the shed. Much to his surprise, there was the moose, five feet away. Larry slowly put the pail down and stepped back. The moose came forward, sniffed the pail curiously, then walked off.

The moose stayed with Jessica, following her around just as he had the first day. By late morning she let him get close enough to nuzzle her. And when she ate, he'd rest his neck on her back and move his head back and forth in a gentle caress.

Later in the day, as Larry went to put hay in the shed for Jessica, he got a feeling . . . a feeling that someone or something was close by, watching him.

He turned around. The moose was just a few feet away. He had appeared without a sound. "Oh brother," thought Larry. "What's going to happen now?" He was afraid an abrupt movement would startle the moose into charging. So he slowly continued putting hay in the shed. The moose observed him a few seconds more (to Larry it seemed like hours), and then walked off and joined Jessica on the other side of the pasture.

After dinner, Larry crossed the road and the moose came to the fence. Larry said, "Hi, big fellow. You sure surprised us by staying another day." He realized he could reach right out and touch the moose. But he thought to himself, "He's a wild animal, and I shouldn't try to encourage him or do anything to domesticate him." He remembered stories he'd read that when you touch a wild animal you are taking that wildness away, so he decided he would not touch the moose.

That evening Larry phoned the State Game Warden, Don Gallus, from nearby Mount Holly. He told him about the moose and asked him to have a look in the morning if the moose were still there. Larry wanted assurance that the moose was healthy and safe, and that he wouldn't harm his animals or anyone else.

Around noon, Larry came home and told Lila he had arranged for a leave of absence from his job. Then he joined Mr. Gallus, who reported that the moose appeared to be in good health, even though it was unusual for one to let people get so close.

After watching the moose for several more hours, Mr. Gallus told Larry he saw no need to tranquilize the moose to move him. He didn't appear to be dangerous and seemed quite content where he was. Mr. Gallus also thought that Larry was treating the moose kindly, not fencing him in or bothering him. There was no fence in the woods at the back of the property, and the pasture fence was only an electric wire eighteen inches off the ground. The moose's long legs, evolved for standing in deep water or snow, could easily carry him over.

Every day from then on "was like a new thing," according to Larry. "I'd get up early and look out and say, 'Is he there?' And Lila would say no. Then by the time I'd get coffee and all, I'd look out the window and say, 'Here he comes.'" Some days the moose was in the woods browsing, his antlered head reaching high in the branches for food. Other days he'd be in the pasture, nosing after Jessica.

In the evenings Larry would go to the pasture, and the moose would come over to the fence and stretch his neck out. "How or why did you pick us?" Larry would ask him softly. "I'm glad you're here and that you're healthy, even if we can't explain your actions."

Larry watched the moose every day and got to know his routine. After browsing early in the morning, he would follow Jessica around. When she tired of him, she would seek solitude under a pine tree with branches so low that the moose couldn't follow without tangling his antlers. He would content himself with standing a few feet away, gazing longingly at her while waiting for her to come out. Sometimes when she came out, she would go right over to him.

The moose had a favorite spot to drink from in the pasture. He found a small shallow pool fed by an underground spring. To get his mouth to the water, he had to kneel down on his long front legs. Sometimes after a snowfall, instead of drinking from the spring, he would eat snow.

Nearly every day the moose found a low bush or shrub, and hooked and rubbed his antlers on it. It is what moose do in the fall, to help scrape the dried velvet off. Now this shadow-boxing developed strength in the moose's neck and shoulder muscles that he could use to combat rivals.

Larry gave him a private name and used it when they talked. "Thank you for coming back, Josh," Larry told him each morning. "I'm so glad to see you again. And when you leave, if you ever pass this way again, even for a moment, please give me some kind of sign or whatever, so I know it's you."

Larry knew that once the moose shed his antlers, it would be very difficult to tell him apart from other moose. He had noticed one other distinctive marking, however. The moose had a small V-shaped scar above his right eye. Larry thought the moose might have cut himself earlier in the year, perhaps running through the woods, or during the accident or fight that damaged his antler. He hoped that as the moose matured, the scar would stay visible.

Ten days passed, then twenty, and the moose was still there. Word of his visit spread. Newspapers, magazines, radio and television stations sent reporters to cover the story. Mr.

Gallus dropped by several more times, and busloads of school-children, local people, and others who had heard or read about the moose came to see for themselves. Some arrived as early as six in the morning. Others drove up after dark and shined their headlights into the pasture. Everyone found it un-usual and funny and even a little touching that a wild moose had come to court a farmer's cow. They called them The Odd Couple, and called him The Lovesick Moose and The Shrews-bury Moose.

Some people suggested that Larry put up a wooden fence and charge admission. He did exactly the opposite. He cut down the wire at the back of the pasture bordering the woods and turned off the electricity in the rest of the fence. He wanted to be absolutely sure the moose could leave whenever he wished.

Over the next few days, Larry noticed that the moose's rou-tine had changed. At mid-morning and again around three in the afternoon, he would stand near the fence and look long-ingly across the road. Larry would clear a path through the crowd for him to cross. Once on the other side, the moose would head down the old logging road and disappear into the woods for two or three hours.

Larry believed the moose needed to widen his range, since he'd probably eaten all the nourishing shoots and twigs nearby. After browsing for a few hours, he'd cross the road again, join the cattle in the pasture, and lie down to chew his cud, gazing out over the valley.

After a heavy snowfall, Larry thought it might be tiring for the moose to plow through the deep snow. The holiday season was approaching, and Larry's nephew was selling Christmas trees. So Larry cut boughs from the trees and brought them into the pasture when he brought hay for the cattle. Sometimes during the day, the moose would lick the block of salt that Larry put out for the cattle.

In the evenings, the moose acted like the chieftain of the barnyard and herded the cattle up to the hay. Then he would maneuver himself into the group and push hay toward Jessica, as though he wanted to make sure she got her fair share (or more). The moose never ate any of the feed put out for the cattle.

After eating, they would all lie down and chew their cuds, and the moose always lay near Jessica. Around ten at night, he'd get up and cross the road again, heading toward the woods. Sometimes he'd walk toward the far meadow, where the horses were. He always returned around seven in the morning, and Larry and Lila were always overjoyed to see him.

By New Year's Eve, the moose had been on Carrara's Mountain sixty-eight days. Larry and Lila tried to prepare themselves for the end of the moose's rutting season. They knew he would shed his antlers and then probably leave. Charles Willey had told them that when moose lose their antlers, they apparently feel defenseless and retreat to the forest for the rest of the winter.

One late morning, Larry received a phone call at work. It was Lila and his nephew. "Can you come home? Right now? The moose is back and one antler is missing!"

Larry drove home quickly. The moose was in the pasture with the cattle, pushing hay toward them. His head looked lopsided, with a tall, stately antler on one side, and a raw red patch on the other. Even though Larry knew the antler was supposed to come off, he thought the moose looked embarrassed, as though his pride had been diminished and he didn't feel as powerful and noble as before.

As Larry walked into the pasture to put out more hay for the cattle, the moose followed a few feet behind. Wherever

Larry went, "the moose would smell the track where I was and walk right in it. I mean, usually I'd walk in his track, you know; he and I were two individuals. But this last day, he and I were together. He walked in my tracks and followed me." Larry felt that night would probably be the last night he would see the moose. He wondered, "Is he trying to say something to me . . . tell me, you know, this is it."

As Larry stood one footstep from the moose, he thought about their morning and evening talks and the trust that had developed between them. He didn't touch him.

That night, the moose lay down as usual with Jessica and the other cattle. Later he moved closer to the house, right by the porch. Larry tried to stay awake all night, but he dozed off. When he woke up, the moose was no longer by the porch, and Larry couldn't see him in the pasture. Before he went to work, he searched but he didn't find him. Larry left, not expecting the moose to return, yet hoping that he might.

About ten in the morning, Lila received a phone call from a neighbor who lived a mile away. The moose had passed through her barnyard that morning, heading toward Salt Ash Mountain, east of Larry's farm. Both antlers were gone, and he was trotting straight ahead, as though he knew where he was going.

Larry and Lila will be looking for the moose in the fall. They wonder if his antlers will grow in again with one "finger" pointing down, and they hope that the small scar above his right eye will still be there. That way they can be sure.

from A MOOSE FOR JESSICA

Buffalo Games

GARY PAULSEN

[EDITORS' NOTE: *During the Iditarod, the dogsled race across Alaska, a rookie driver came upon a musher who had stopped his team and was gazing down a hill with rapt attention. The rookie driver stopped to see what the other man found so absorbing.*]

We were looking down on a frozen lake—one of the Farewell Lakes. But it wasn't the lake that held his interest. Below and to the right, a group of four buffalo were standing on the shore. Two of them were in the grass at the edge and the other two were out on the ice.

"Somebody told me that there was a herd of buffalo here, but I hadn't expected to see them along the trail," he said.

"Yes," I told the other musher. "Buffalo. I know. They told us . . ."

"No—*watch.*"

I turned back, thinking frankly that he was around the bend. So it was buffalo—so what?

Then I saw what he meant.

The surface of the lake was bare of snow and the two buffalo out on the ice were having a rough time of it trying to stand. One of the buffalo on the shore backed away from the lake, up the sloping side of the ridge, pawed the ground a couple of times and ran full bore for the lake.

Just as he hit the edge of the ice, his tail went straight up in the air. He spread his front feet apart, stiffened his legs and slid away from shore, spinning around in a circle as he flew across the ice.

When he slowed to a stop he bellowed, a kind of "Gwaaa" sound, then began making his tortuous way back to the shoreline.

While he was doing this, the fourth buffalo came shooting out on the ice, slid farther (also tail up) than the last, made a louder noise, and started back slipping and falling.

I couldn't believe it and blinked rapidly several times, thinking I was hallucinating.

"No—it's real," he laughed. "I was passing when I heard the bellow and came up to check it out. I've been here an hour, maybe a little more. They've been doing this the whole time. Great, isn't it?"

We lay there for another half-hour watching them play. The object seemed to be who could slide the farthest, and each of them tried several times, tails up, happy bellows echoing on the far shore of the lake as they slid across the ice.

Buffalo Games...who would have thought it could happen?

from WINTERDANCE
(as excerpted in CHICKEN SOUP FOR THE PET LOVER'S SOUL)

In the Sky

"*A wise old owl sat on an oak,*
The more he saw the less he spoke."

EDWARD HERSEY RICHARDS

$\mathcal{S}$ometimes we forget that our world consists of more than the earth beneath our feet—until we follow the flight of a bird up into the sky. Or watch one come out of nowhere to perch on a feeder hanging from a tree. People have always been inspired by sky creatures and wished they could follow them up into the air. But even if we can't, we're grateful for their presence because they remind us that God has blessed us with so many wonderful creatures. And they encourage us to look beyond the space we live in.

A Big, Ugly Baby

JENNIFER OWINGS DEWEY

On a cold, bright New Mexico morning I awoke to a familiar sound, a hoarse croaking that broke the stillness of the early day. At once I knew what it was and who it was. It was Clem, the raven.

Only a few weeks earlier Clem had flown off for what I supposed would be the last time. He had been leaving in the afternoons and staying away all night more and more frequently. Then for several days he did not return at all. Now here he was. Back again.

I went outside and looked up. The air was clear. High overhead a dark shape traced wide circles in the sky. I shaded my eyes with my hand and watched Clem's wings rise and fall. His powerful head hung down a little, and his huge beak was slightly open.

His wings carried him up and around, then into a long, smooth glide toward the ground.

Ravens build nests in trees, on cliffs, or sometimes in abandoned buildings, using hundreds of sticks. In places where sticks are hard to find, they use the bones of dead animals, or even baling or barbed wire. Fur, deer hair, moss, grass—any soft debris—becomes their nest lining.

43

Clem's mother had built her nest near the top of a pine tree, where it had little shelter from gusting winds. Late in the spring a fierce storm had ripped the nest apart, plunging four nestlings to the forest floor. A hiker discovers the accident a few hours later. Near the base of the tree, on the ground, lay three lifeless baby ravens. A fourth sat shivering, almost out of sight under a bush. The hiker brings the fourth baby raven home in the bowl of his hat. The hiker is my husband, Keith.

Ravens are big birds. Full grown, they stand as tall as a large house cat and weigh about two pounds. I have never seen a baby raven before. This baby is a damp, almost feather-less handful, stunned and miserable, weighing less than a pound. Its wrinkled, raw-looking skin is dotted with patchy tufts of down and a few twisted, rumpled feathers. About six inches long, as wide as my hand when I make a fist, its bony body looks like it would fall apart if its skin didn't hold it together.

Keith and I know enough about birds to recognize this wet baby as a raven. But we need to know more. We look ravens up in the bird guide: Common Raven, member of the crow family, subfamily Corvinae. Other relatives are rooks, nutcrackers, jackdaws, and crows. From the down on its upper body, and the few crumpled feathers growing at odd angles out of its wings, we judge it to be about two weeks old.

We name the baby Clem almost immediately. We like the sound of the name and it is easy to say. When we name him we agree it will be all right if he turns out to be "Clementine."

Clem is all head, stomach, and enormous beak. His body looks too large for his skinny legs. He cannot stand up, and fluttering his wings makes his head wobble. A thin bluish membrane half closes over his eyes every now and then. (This membrane is called the "third eyelid" in adult birds, and protects the eyes in flight.) When I hold Clem cupped in my hands I feel the rhythm of his heart beating against his chest.

His beak is a translucent whitish-gray, like wax paper. Inside his beak, along the upper edge, the bluish-gray turns to bright yellow. A thick red tongue shaped like a cone moves forward and back when Clem's beak is open. (As a brand-new baby, Clem's beak is open most of the time.) Looking down his throat I feel I can see all the way to his stomach.

Right from the start we love this big, ugly baby. And right from the start he loves us back.

After drying Clem off we line a cardboard box with a soft, woolly scarf and pieces of old towels. Clem appears to accept this substitute nest. Perhaps the high sheltering sides of the box remind him of his original home.

Resting gently on the bottom, Clem relaxes. His eyelids close over his eyes, his head drops on his chest, and he sleeps. We begin to think about what to feed him.

We know wild ravens eat almost anything, so we decide to offer Clem a variety of foods to take the place of the insects, worms, and carrion his real mother would give him. There is no need to be delicate about feeding this baby bird, no need for eyedroppers or other special devices to coax food down his throat.

After twenty or thirty minutes of sleep Clem awakens and he squawks vigorously, his beak open as far as it will go, his eyes imploring: FEED ME! We do—bread soaked in milk, dog food softened in warm water, crumbled hard-boiled eggs. He loves milk-toast with honey, Mandarin orange segments, and pinto beans. Whatever the food, we simply hold it over Clem's open beak and drop it in, three to twelve meals a day, round the clock.

He seems not to swallow. The food disappears into his enormous maw and reappears almost immediately at the tail end. We can watch its progress, since there are so few feathers covering his skin. The lumps pass through at breakneck speed. Is it our imagination or does he eject more than he takes in? This is impossible. Somehow he gains nourishment, despite his rapid-fire digestive system. Hunger calls, loud, long and pitiful, turn to low, soft gurgles once Clem's stomach is "filled."

For the first three days, Clem does little but sleep and eat, eat and sleep. He sleeps for three or four hours and then is ready to be fed again. This goes on morning and night. His sounds tell us what state he is in: hungry, satisfied, or somewhere between one and the other.

Clem's Latin name is *Corvus corax*. We read that *corax* comes from the Greek work *korax,* meaning "a croaker." A fitting name for this baby raven. He can make soft, gentle sounds or ear-piercing screeches. His sounds are not birdsong—raven sounds are more language than song.

Wild ravens communicate with a wide repertoire of croaks, gurgles, growls, coos, caws, screeches, screams, cackles, and rattles. There are alarm calls, assembly calls, mating, and scolding calls. Flocks have identifying calls, and so do individuals. Bursts of caws, usually six or seven to a burst, short or long, with varying pauses between, establish identifying patterns. Messages are being passed.

Clem communicates to us with coos and grunts—rumbles of sounds that seem to come from his belly, not his vocal cords. Within a few days of his arrival we recognize patterns and repetitions. His urgent "CAWCAWCAW!!" announces he is hungry. His "CROAKCROAKCROAK" tells us he is happy for the moment. A series of soft gurgles tells us he is drifting off to sleep.

We wonder: what does a baby raven want? What does it need? We wonder what a real mother raven and nestlings provide that we have no hope of providing. We decide, without thinking about it consciously, to raise him. He would not survive in the wild. There are too many dogs, cats, and other dangers for one so defenseless as Clem. We talk about how to keep such an unusual pet. We agree it will be best to keep him free. We will not clip his wings, nor keep him caged. We will allow him access to the real world.

The first ten days Clem spends in or near his box. He is content to be lifted out by hand and placed gently on the floor. Much of the time he is groggy, even stupid. His insatiable appetite rules him. Empty, he screeches for food, full, he sleeps a deep and satisfied sleep. We watch him—and with gleaming blue-black eyes he watches us. We listen to his wet, gurgling croaks, and we wonder; does he dream? Do baby birds have thoughts? How difficult it is not to assume things about him.

On a diet of all sorts of unbirdfood-like things, Clem grows. We feed him bananas, vanilla pudding, applesauce, and strawberries. Keith holds Clem on his knee, securing him with one large hand. Bulky and black, feathered like a pincushion, Clem tips his head back, opens his beak, and Keith drops bits of ripe, mashed banana down his throat. Clem accepts the firm grip of Keith's hand.

Clumps of grayish-brown down fall out, and feathers grow in on Clem's wings, chest, and sides. At first his feathers appear in rows, like stripes on a uniform. In between the rows is wrinkled, naked skin. Tailfeathers also grow. These are half as long as his adult tailfeathers will be, but they help him keep his balance when he hops across the floor, which he tries to do within five days of his arrival. He flutters his wings, loses his balance, tries again. Finally he hops without falling over. These first journeys never take him far—and he almost always has to be carried back to his box.

Clem is curious. Like a pond beetle sensitive to surface changes in light and motion, once out of his box he becomes increasingly alert to anything new in the room. If it is something small, he notices it. If it is something big, he reacts. A tiny bug blown in on the breeze, a human visitor, a moth fluttering in a corner—Clem wants to investigate.

Unsteady on his legs, a drunken sailor of a bird weaving his way from one place to another, Clem begins to explore his world. . . .

The season turns and we work longer hours, knowing winter to be near. We stack bales of alfalfa from the fields, to be sold as feed during the coming winter. We shuck corn and pick apples. I make apple butter over an outdoor fire, spooning and stirring the hot, sweet-smelling mixture around and around in a big pot. The air smells ripe.

Late September. Harvest time. Clem begins to walk off and require rescue many times a day. It is a nuisance to have to stop everything and follow calls from the wayward raven.

Each time one of us goes to find him he is in a tree, or a bush, or sitting forlornly on the ground, mussed-up and unhappy. His behavior perplexes us: Why is he so jittery and frightened? We decide to sit and watch him for a while.

This is what we see: Clem beats his wings, now full-feathered and strong. They slap and flap vigorously. He dances around on his feet as if on hot ground. Hopping forward, wings up, wings down, hopping faster and faster, each hop taking him farther than the previous hop—each hop less of a landing—

until, finally, he leaves the ground completely and is airborne.

These first tries end in a variety of ways.

One way he lands abruptly on his stomach after a very short flight, his wings useless appendages. In another, he gains height and distance only to have it appear he has failed to consider direction. He turns sharply in the air, loses momentum, throws his wings straight up, and plummets to earth like a stone. Sometimes he gets quite high in the air—higher than the roof of the house—but seems to lose courage. Looking down he forgets to flap his wings. Again he falls to the ground in a heap, his breath knocked away.

We live on flat land, the trees nicely spaced with bushes in between, an ideal place for a young raven to learn to fly. Lots of room for long takeoffs and gentle, gliding landings.

Clem manages to miss all the soft spots, sail right past the best bushes, crash land instead of float down, and end up exhausted, tousled, and screeching. Fortunately his calls carry. I hear him, and, looking all around, I finally see a tiny, black spot creating a commotion in a distant bush or tree.

His landings in trees are especially troublesome to us. If the tree cannot be climbed there is always the ladder. But sometimes the ladder is half a mile away, or more. One time I shimmy up a tree, coax Clem to a lower branch where I can grab him, reach for what I think is a substantial part of him, and end up with a fistful of feathers. Clem lands on the ground, unhurt but furious.

Landings in bushes are simply a matter of untangling raven feathers and limbs from branches and leaves.

After these crashes Clem needs consolation, comfort, and reassurance. We carry him home, speaking gently and petting him.

In the wild Clem would have taken to the air sooner. Learning from his parents, he might have flown a month earlier. With us Clem is a late bloomer. With us Clem has it made. He is content to live on the ground for a long while.

Eventually he truly flies. His first successful flight takes him in a wide circle all around our neighborhood, within sight of our house, our yard, of Keith and Tamar and me watching. He learns to do somersaults, rolls, fly upside-down, and land gracefully. His takeoffs remain the least fluid part of his maneuvers. A series of bounding hops, with wings arched up, head stiff, beak a little open, carry him across the ground until (finally) he rises into the air. Takeoffs are especially unwieldy when his belly is full. But after the first success, he always makes it into the air.

We think he might leave us once he knows how to fly.

from CLEM: THE STORY OF A RAVEN

The Return of the Sparrows

FAIRLY CHANDLER

I had gone through a long illness and recovery period and, still unable to work, I found there were many hours in the day when there was little for me to do except fish in the Magnolia River or wander in the woods, things my dad and I had once done together.

While I was out in the woods, I began to notice how many birds there were around me. In the spring and fall especially, as the birds moved north and south with the change of seasons, there would be birds everywhere.

Sometimes these migrants would encounter a storm out in the Gulf and would fight to get out of the winds that blew them off their course; and they'd be so weary from battling the weather, they'd light at their first landfall, which would be Dauphin Island, to the west of me, or Fort Morgan, to the south. Then there would be unimaginable numbers and species everywhere, so exhausted and desperate for food and water you could walk among them and almost pick them up.

Having spent a lot of time in the woods when I was a boy in northern Alabama, I thought I knew birds, but I was seeing birds I'd never seen before and couldn't identify. So I got some books and I started reading up on them. The more I read and observed, the more fascinated I became.

I learned there are some 350 species that appear in Alabama. Of the whole family of warblers, for example, about forty species nest, winter, or migrate through coastal Alabama where I live. Some nest as far north as the Arctic and winter as far south as Central and South America. But they all pass through Alabama going south in fall and north again in spring.

And they're in different plumages when they come. Some change plumage completely from spring to fall and back to spring.

By now I had bought myself some binoculars so I could get a better look at the birds, and I found it wasn't all that difficult. Generally, birds aren't as secretive as many wild animals— a fox or rabbit or snake, for instance. Birds are active during the day, and most of them are out in the open, where they can be seen.

The next thing was for me to get out my cameras and photographic equipment and start taking pictures of the birds. I had been a fashion photographer in New York until my health failed and I was forced to return to my parents' home in Alabama. Now I was able to combine my new interest with the one that had been my profession.

You've got to get pretty close to a bird to get a decent picture of it—a whole lot closer than a bird watcher with binoculars needed to be—and as I got nearer, I began seeing more.

One bird I noticed, the cerulean warbler, had his habitat high in the treetops, and that was where I'd always find him, a small blue bird sometimes hard to spot because he was up so high. The black-and-white warbler had his habitat in the large limbs of the hardwood trees. The yellow-throated warbler's habitat was farther out on those same limbs. The brown-headed nuthatch was always in the pines, on the limbs and sometimes on the trunk.

Each bird had his own assigned place, and that was where his food was to be found. The nits and spiders and spider eggs that the brown creeper ate, for example, were on the trunk of the tree, so that was his place.

It was astounding, I thought, the way each bird was taken care of, guided and given its role in life, as if according to some master plan.

Another thing I found remarkable was the way each bird, with very few exceptions, followed exactly the plan for its life, completely obedient and trusting that when it did what it was supposed to do, was in the place where it was supposed to be at the time when it was supposed to be there, all its needs would be taken care of. And, I noticed, they were.

I couldn't help contrasting the birds' behavior with my own. I had been practically a vegetable for a number of years and became physically and financially exhausted and sick with anxiety over how I would take care of myself. Earlier, when the pain was so bad I could hardly stand it and I was so weak I could hardly move, I believed I'd never be able to get out of bed, sometimes that I'd never see another dawn. And yet, I had.

During this time I observed something in the bird world that gave me one of the most important lessons I now believe God knew I needed.

I had become curious about the white-throated sparrows that spent a large part of the winter in my backyard. I had read that all white-throated sparrows nest along the Great Lakes and up into Canada, and I was interested in finding out how long those birds lived, where in Canada they nested, what kind of routes they took between Alabama and Canada, and when they left to come south.

So I trapped and banded a number of them, placing on their legs small, aluminum bands bearing numbers that would identify those particular birds. I released the birds and when they headed north once more, I began waiting hopefully for notification that someone, a thousand miles or more away, perhaps far into northern Ontario, had spotted "my" sparrows.

That notification would come from the U.S. Fish and Wildlife Service to which I had reported the band numbers and other information. If one of my sparrows were sighted and its band recovered, the finder would report the information concerning it, and the information would, through a computer system, make its way to and through the Fish and Wildlife Service and eventually to me.

I waited and waited. Summer came and went. As the days slipped by, I knew the sparrows would soon feel the first chill of Canadian autumn and begin to fly southward again.

Near the middle of October, when I still hadn't heard any word, I gave up on those birds, at least for that year, guessing I'd just have to band a few more when they came for another winter in my yard.

By November, as sure and predictable as the seasons themselves, white-throated sparrows were filling my backyard again. I set out my trap.

That was when I made an amazing discovery. Among the birds I succeeded in catching were a number of sparrows I had banded the previous winter! Uncanny!

Flying over more than a thousand miles, these tiny sparrows had managed to find the same shrub in my backyard where they had wintered a year earlier, one bush among millions, over hundreds of square miles of trees and bushes, guided by some inexplicable set of directions planted in their little brains. Remarkable!

Suddenly something lighted in my own head. It was something Jesus had said about sparrows, words I'd pondered before.

"Are not two sparrows sold for a penny?" Jesus said. "And not one of them will fall to the ground without your Father's will. . . . Fear not, therefore; you are of more value than many sparrows." (Matthew 10:29,31, RSV)

Then I remembered the night when I was so desperately anxious about where the money was going to come from to take care of me and my mother after my dad died. I had slid out of bed and fallen to my knees on the bedroom floor and prayed to a God I hadn't known, pleading for help.

I remembered how swiftly help had come, when some worthless shares in a defunct business suddenly turned out to be worth enough to see us through for a long time to come.

I remembered how, despite my having given up, I had been brought through years of invalidism.

I remembered that even while I had wondered how I could survive, a new successful treatment had been developed and made available to me.

I remembered how, confined to the house and yard for so long, with little purpose to my life, I had been given the beauty of the birds to study and photograph.

"Having eyes do you not see . . . ?" Jesus had said. "And do you not remember?" (Mark 8:18, RSV)

Yes, I could see. It was clear that God had been in my life all along, loving and providing for me no less than He did for all His creatures. I would try to remember that.

And now, especially when I get up close to the birds, it's

more obvious than ever to me that His eye *is* on the sparrow, and I know He watches over me and blesses me as I learn to love and trust and serve Him according to His marvelous plan.

The Hemlock Pair

JEAN CRAIGHEAD GEORGE

The wind twisted the white feathers on the heads of two magnificent bald eagles, the national emblem of the United States of America. Their yellow eyes were focused on two men crouched in their eight-by-ten-foot stick nest in an oak tree on the shore of Hemlock Lake in northwestern New York. The eagles cried in alarm.

Eagles mate for life. This pair, known as the Hemlock Pair, had raised young together for more than twenty years. This day in their big nest was one egg, which unbeknownst to them, was contaminated with chemicals. It would never hatch.

It was the year 1977, and the bald eagle was almost extinct in the eastern United States, primarily due to the chemicals ingested in their food. One of the chemicals, DDT, caused eagle eggs to be infertile or to crumble. Cities and highways deprived them of home sites.

The two men were part of the New York State Bald Eagle Recovery Program, the first such program in the United States. When they left the eagle nest that day, the Hemlock Pair circled overhead and disappeared.

Four days later, the eagles returned to find their egg gone and two eggs in its place. The men had removed the infertile egg and replaced it with hawk eggs. A bird must go through the period of incubation to get its parental hormones flowing strongly enough to feed and brood young. The men hoped the eagles would incubate the hawk eggs; then, at the right moment, they would replace them with a live eaglet. The plan never got that far. The eagles saw the strange eggs and deserted the nest.

The next year the female laid another polluted egg. After the Hemlock Pair had been incubating it for almost a month, the men climbed back to the nest for a few minutes, then quickly departed.

When the Hemlock Pair returned, they found a two-and-a-half-week old bald eagle chick staring up at them. "Tarzan," as the men called him, had been hatched by captive eagles at the U.S. Fish and Wildlife Service's Patuxent Wildlife Research Center in Maryland. His worth could not be calculated. He was the hope of the many people trying to return the bald eagle to the American skies. Tarzan looked up at his foster parents, opened his beak and begged for food.

That did it. The hungry baby inspired the Hemlock Pair to pluck morsels from a fish they had stored and stuff the open mouth. Seeing that, the men stole away. The Hemlock Pair were going to be good parents.

They were right. In late June, Tarzan spread his huge wings and sailed out over the lake and hills to independence. He was the first bald eaglet to be fledged from a wild nest in New York in five years.

The next year, the recovery team brought two eaglets to the nest too soon. The pair were not ready to feed and brood young, and they abandoned two eaglets. The men did not give up. A few days later they put a dummy egg in the nest. The pair looked at it, rolled it, then took turns incubating. In April they were ready to nurture, and when the men placed another eaglet in their nest, they raised it to independence.

In 1981 tragedy struck. The Hemlock male was shot. The recovery team was about to abandon their foster parent program when, in mid-March, the female surprised them by bringing home a new mate. He was a banded eagle from another New York State recovery program. He took up his duties as father, and together the two raised eight foster eaglets in the next several years.

When the female died at about thirty years of age, the male found a new mate. DDT had been banned for almost ten years, and this female was not polluted. That year a completely new Hemlock Pair laid fertile eggs and fledged healthy young. The men's work was done. Wild eagles were raising wild eaglets again.

from ANIMALS WHO HAVE WON OUR HEARTS

Mama Robin

BARBARA EARL THOMAS

The birds were plentiful that spring. The air thick with sparrows, starlings, low-flying crows, and fabulously fat robins. Since the vines around my porch had finally started to thicken, it seemed that the birds approached ever more closely, swirling, dipping, and then lighting to pick at invisible insects or to drink from the moisture trapped on the leaves. One morning after I turned to enter the house, after inspecting my seeding flower bed, a robin squawked as I opened the screen door. Startled, I looked up to find her aloft in the corner, perched on the edge of my hanging fuchsia basket. Amidst the foilage I could make out her profile, a solid inflated form out of which stared one piercing black eye. For some moments I stood transfixed by her. But I could see no evidence for her protest. I broke our gaze, went in, and gave it no further thought.

In the week that followed, I noticed her again and again. She squawked upon my entrance or exit. With each squawk her glare intensified. I just stared back. The longer I held her defiant gaze, the more she puffed up. I began to anticipate her presence and that annoying commotion. Like an official announcement, it heralded my comings and goings, and affirmed my presence. When she was away from the basket, I wondered, I'm here, so where are you? Come announce me, pierce me with your black eye.

I took to watching and waiting for the bird. Once I was able to pick her out from among the several in the yard, I noticed that she was not always alone. At times she was accompanied in her daily activities by another smaller robin. I watched them come and go in and out of the vine, rustling it as they went. They appeared content to have me there as long as I remained still. They never flew directly into the vine. One or the other might stop first on the telephone wire, then cautiously move to the magnolia just south of the porch, then on to the rosebush and then furtively move onto the vine. They came carrying in their beaks twigs and other bits of debris. By now, I knew their secret: They were building a nest somewhere in the upper corner of my vine. I looked for it, at first casually and then with determination. For days its location eluded me until, while watering my hanging fuchsia basket, I spied an unusual formation at the base of the plant's branch structure. It was a weaving in and out, a soft scooped-out cup, a construction in progress.

After a brief moment of triumph, panic set in. What was wrong with these birds? Where were their instincts? Why did they pick this hanging basket, and not a tree, on a porch within eye and earshot of humans? I could only imagine that these birds are just like us, pushed by the pressures of an ever-speeding world until they had lost their intuition. I surmised they had picked the porch because the overhang provided protection from low-swooping crows, and the plant because it offered so much foliage and the branches formed a perfect warp for weaving a nest. But without water it would soon not be an ideal hiding space. If the nest was going to be there I had to somehow figure out how to water the plant. And furthermore, if we were all going to be out there on the porch together, the bird was going to have to stop all that squawking every time I walked in and out of the door. After all, it was my porch first.

With the construction of the nest completed, the two bird flights in and out of the vine waned, and the job of tending it fell, at last, to the one that had so abruptly caught my eye some weeks ago. If my fat bird friend, whom I had taken to calling Mama Bird, squawked when I was outside, I'd talk to her out loud. I'd say, "Hey, pipe down, no one's done anything to you yet and you've been here for weeks. And besides, you made this decision, so live with it!" This must have seemed reasonable, for she soon quieted down and just sat in motionless profile when I appeared. She even let me water the plant on the side away from the nest with my long-spouted watering can, but she always kept that one black eye trained on me.

On a day when Mama Bird happened to be away, I ventured carefully up on the ledge of the porch to peer down into the hanging basket. While I knew that the eggs would be there, I was surprised and touched to actually see them. There they were, three tiny eggs of the most delicate translucent blue I had ever seen. They glowed and in their translucence appeared to be floating just above the nest that held them. I moved quietly away and down. It was too much. I began to wish again that she had done it in a tree.

In the days that followed, Mama Bird and I fashioned a set of rules that allowed us to be on the porch together. I agreed not to bustle too near her nesting station and she came to understand the futility of her wild squawking. But that eye of hers, to which I had now grown accustomed, maintained its strict surveillance, keeping me in line lest I forget myself and somehow offend. It grew hard to imagine what a fuchsia could look like without a fat robin burrowed in amongst its branches. I began to think that hanging pots should come with birds to nest in them.

I must admit I wasn't actually looking forward to these pink-eyed, naked chicks chirping for worms. I'm a worrier. I worry about everything. I was just at the point of hyperventilation when I heard her trill, and caught sight of her circuitous approach. From treetop, to rosebush, to vine, Mama Bird traveled back with her beak full of a dark, wiggling mass. The pink ones met her return with jubilation and a bobbing-headed joy. I could see them there, all three of them with their beaks stretched open, instinctively begging. So this is how it's done. I thought I should water the lawn and even open the compost bin, that was always full of worms. Maybe I could even scoop out a few rich shovelfuls and bring them around so she wouldn't have to fly so far.

When Mama Bird was not feeding the chicks, she was sitting on top of her brood to keep them warm. They grew fast. At feeding time I could easily see their heads above the ridge of the nest. I was now in the habit of checking each morning and night to see if my fat robin was there at her station. In the evening before bed I viewed it as a good omen when I was able to make out her profile, sitting steady and solid on her nest, ready to pass the night.

On one of these nights I was awakened by the most piercing, mournful shrill I had ever heard. It was the sound of terror. It surrounded me, filling the room. It entered my bones and I bolted upright. I knew in an instant that it was the bird. She was there, just beyond my bedroom window, beating her wings furiously against the gutter, which echoed her shrieking. Like a shot I was up and out of the bed with my husband close on my heels.

In an instant I was on the porch. To my horror I found a big, yellow, thick-necked tomcat seated snugly in the middle of the fuchsia basket. He had one bird in his mouth. The two others had fallen down onto the porch floor and were there stumbling about. In shock and disbelief, I waved my arms wildly and screamed at the cat to get out! Get out! In response the cat just turned its head calmly and eyed me as if I was the most absurd creature it had ever encountered.

Seeing the predicament, my husband quickly jumped up onto the ledge and forcibly extracted the cat by the scruff of the neck, flinging him to the porch. Upon hitting the ground, the cat shook its head, dropped its prey and shot me one last confused glance before retreating into the night with baby bird on his breath.

By this time the neighbors on either side were out in their yards wondering who had been burglarized, or worse, murdered. I remember only briefly acknowledging their presence before my attention trained on the calamity at hand. Two birds were still wobbling around while the mama bird moaned somewhere not far off. The carcass of the third lay lifeless on the edge of the stair leading out to the yard. I thought I saw my husband make a motion as if he were going to pick up one of the birds. Now I was shrieking. Don't touch them! Don't touch them! Somewhere in my bungled brain I remembered hearing that parent birds wouldn't care for their young if they were touched by human hands.

My first thought was to take down the plant holding the nest to see if I might coerce the chicks to jump up into it. Upon looking again at the terrified, weary little creatures, I immediately thought better of that plan. In a flash I found myself in the kitchen, looking around for some helpful tool. What I chose was a large ladle-like soup spoon. Back out on the porch, instrument in hand, I swooped down and presented the spoon at the feet of one of the little birds. Without hesitation, to my amazement, it jumped right into the spoon as if it were the elevator it had been waiting for all of its little bird life. I lifted it quickly and carefully back up into the nest. The second baby followed suit.

I anxiously awaited Mama Bird's return the next day. I watched and worried. Several times I found myself just standing in front of the window or out on the porch, willing myself to see her familiar shape. The waiting was long and painful. It was unbearable to consider that I might have saved the chicks from the cat only to have them die of exposure and hunger. I imagined Mama Bird on some nearby branch weighing her options and watching me with those black robin eyes.

I, too, was weighing my options, none of which seemed the least bit reasonable. While not impossible, the idea of climbing up to the nest several times a day with worms had absolutely no appeal. I vacillated between being desperate and morose. When I finally could stand it no longer I went out onto the porch and called to her in a high-pitched singsong voice, chanting, Mama Birdie, Mama Birdie, over and over—willing her to take up her place once more in the fuchsia.

As the day wore on I resigned myself to the difficult task ahead and the reality of the poor prospects for my brood. I scolded myself for not having anticipated the possible dangers.

With dusk at hand, I was at the point of conceding when I heard a movement and bustle from the basket. It was too much to hope for, I thought. I feared that my wanting had finally driven me to hallucinations, a conjuring of phantom birds. But no, it was true. It was her solid robin-self, briskly surveying the damage and checking the babies. She was back! Like a condemned man reprieved, I was filled with such joy I could barely contain myself.

This was a second chance, rarely granted, and with it I would not fail or be caught off guard by natural, or any other, predators. I staked out the porch. What we needed was a gentle but effective barrier, an early warning system, or a moat perhaps filled with water. My solution was to gather up all the available buckets and jars, fill them with water and place them all around the porch and along the ledge leading up to the nest. This obstacle course was meant to impede and confuse any predatory approach. Cats trying to make their way up to the nest would either fall into the pails, which would make them so crazy they would leave, or knock over the jars, in which case I would hear them and come running.

The next step was to move my sleeping quarters from the second to the first floor. I convinced my husband that we should sleep on the sofa bed with the front door ajar until the birds completed their nesting. After all, one could hardly maintain a vigil sleeping upstairs a floor away. The final piece of the plan called for one of us to be at the house at all times. It was too stressful to leave the house thinking I might find dead birds upon returning.

Who can guess what Mama Bird made of it all. But in truth I sensed that she went about raising the two remaining chicks with a renewed energy. Perhaps she, too, was joyously living her second chance, having escaped nature's odds. And, while she continued to keep close watch on me and all else sur-

rounding her porch, I swear that black eye of hers had lost its
opaque darkness. It had become instead a dark liquid pool that
shone. It no longer nailed me or shut me out. Now, when she
held my gaze, it included me in its reflection as something necessary and natural to her home on the porch.

Mama Bird chirped and sang as she flew in and out to the
chicks who were no longer the pink-beige things I had spied
only weeks before. They were now gawky preteen downy birds,
starting to show their first signs of feathers. Although Mama
Bird continued to bring food in, she seemed to do so less frequently, and at times she would sit in the little tree just across
from the porch in full sight of the nest and sing to the young
ones, who grew excited and implored her to feed them.

Around this time I rarely left the house. I knew that soon I
would see their first flight. Now and then she would arrive
without worms, and the teen birds would flap their wings and
move about in great agitation. She would groom them and
then fly to her perch in the tree just across from the nest. As
she sat in the tree watching her brood and they watching her, I
heard a distinctly different ring to her song. It was a low, reso-
nant, melodious coo that seemed to come from some place
deep inside her chest. It was cajoling, and it drew the birds up
onto the edge of the nest, flapping their wings.

One and then the other would take its place at the edge of
the nest. Testing for flight, they would jump up, teeter, flap
their wings awkwardly, and eventually fall back into the nest,
seemingly exhausted or hoping that Mama Bird would see
their difficulty and just bring them their food. But she just continued her song, low and sweetly, "It is your time, it is your
time, you must come, you must come."

All of this I watched for hours from my station out beyond

the porch, beyond the driveway, crouched low, sitting, watching, and waiting. Each new attempt drew my silent urging in consort with Mama Bird for them to go up and out. I dared not even go to the bathroom.

Finally the bigger of the two birds made his most courageous effort. He unfolded his wings, and stretching them, he went even further than before. He pulled himself up and out as if unwrapping to become a larger bird. It was as though the timer of his instinct had just gone off, and he knew something now that only moments before he hadn't. Once more he mounted the edge of the nest. With wings in motion, he chirped to Mama Bird. She, in return, cooed low and soft, steadily imploring, imploring. In measured response, a loosened grip, an edging forward in one last tilt that almost looked like falling, the bird flew off.

Having held my breath, for how long I could not say, I gasped and lunged slightly forward. With my heart pumping the sound of oceans through my ears, time stood still, all was silent witness, and one flight stood out from among countless first flights taken.

from SWEET HOPE WAITING (INTIMATE NATURE)

The Pigeon Race

ERNEST THOMPSON SETON

We passed through the side door of a big stable on West Nineteenth Street. The mild smell of the well-kept stalls was lost in the sweet odor of hay, as we mounted a ladder and entered the long garret. The south end was walled off, and the familiar "Coo-oo, cooooo-oo, ruk-at-a-coo," varied with the "whirr, whirr, whirr" of wings, informed us that we were at the pigeon-loft.

This was the home of a famous lot of birds, and today there was to be a race among fifty of the youngsters. The owner of the loft had asked me, as an unprejudiced outsider, to be judge in the contest.

It was a training race of the young birds. They had been taken out for short distances with their parents once or twice, then set free to return to the loft. Now for the first time they were to be flown without the old ones. The point of start, Elizabeth, N.J., was a long journey for their first unaided attempt. "But then," the trainer remarked, "that's how we weed out the fools; only the best birds make it, and that's all we want back."

There was another side to the flight. It was to be a race among those that did return. Each of the men about the loft as well as several neighboring fanciers were interested in one or other of the Homers. They made up a purse for the winner, and on me was to devolve the important duty of deciding which should take the stakes. Not the first bird *back,* but the first bird *into the loft,* was to win, for one that returns to his neighborhood merely, without immediately reporting at home, is of little use as a letter-carrier.

The Homing Pigeon used to be called the Carrier because it carried messages, but here I found that name restricted to the show bird, the creature with absurdly developed wattles; the one that carries the messages is now called the Homer, or Homing Pigeon—the bird that always comes home. These Pigeons are not of any special color, nor have they any of the fancy adornments of the kind that figure in Bird shows. They are not bred for style, but for speed and for their mental gifts. They must be true to their home, able to return to it without fail. The sense of direction is now believed to be located in the bony labyrinth of the ear. There is no creature with finer sense of locality and direction than a good Homer, and the only visible proofs of it are the great bulge on each side of the head over the ears, and the superb wings that complete his equipment to obey the noble impulse of home-love. Now the mental and physical equipments of the last lot of young birds were to be put to test.

Although there were plenty of witnesses, I thought it best to close all but one of the pigeon-doors and stand ready to shut that behind the first arrival.

I shall never forget the sensations of that day. I had been warned: "They start at 12; they should be here at 12:30; but look out, they come like a whirlwind. You hardly see them till they're in."

We were ranged along the inside of the loft, each with an

eye to a crack or a partly closed pigeon-door, anxiously scan-
ning the southwestern horizon, when one shouted: "Look
out—here they come!" Like a white cloud they burst into view,
low skimming over the city roofs, around a great chimney pile,
and in two seconds after first being seen they were back. The
flash of white, the rush of pinions, were all so sudden, so short,
that, though preparing, I was unprepared. I was at the only
open door. A whistling arrow of blue shot in, lashed my face
with its pinions, and passed. I had hardly time to drop the little
door, as a yell burst from the men, "Arnaux! Arnaux! I told you
he would. Oh, he's a darling; only three months old and a winner—he's a little darling!" and Arnaux's owner danced, more
for joy in his bird than in the purse he had won.

The men sat or kneeled and watched him in positive rev-
erence as he gulped a quantity of water, then turned to the
food-trough.

"Look at that eye, those wings, and did you ever see such a
breast? Oh, but he's the real grit!" so his owner prattled to the
silent ones whose birds had been defeated.

That was the first of Arnaux's exploits. Best of fifty birds
from a good loft, his future was bright with promise.

He was invested with the silver anklet of the Sacred Order
of the High Homer. It bore his number, 2590 C, a number
which today means much to all men in the world of the
Homing Pigeon.

from ANIMAL HEROES

Watching the Loons

PAUL REZENDES

$\mathcal{I}$ had taken a job as a loon warden on Quabbin in the spring of 1984. At this time, loons were a species of special concern in Massachusetts, a state in the southernmost part of the loons' breeding range. There were only a handful of loons nesting in the whole state, and there was an effort by the government to make sure those loons succeeded in breeding and producing chicks.

Quabbin had several nest sites to which mated pairs of loons returned each spring after wintering in coastal areas. I had volunteered to watch over those loons, but as often happens when you volunteer for projects, sooner or later you're likely to find yourself hired for a paying job. If you're a good enough volunteer, before you know it, the powers that be realize you're indispensable.

In 1984, loons were in decline over much of the North American continent. They faced many hazards: coexistence on lakes with boats, ingestion of lead sinkers, contamination of fresh water in their breeding grounds, loss of their habitat to development, loss of fish prey to acid precipitation, and fluctuating water levels on lakes managed for electric power or for drinking water. . . .

Loons have a certain power and mystique, to which I am

not immune. They're one of the most ancient birds in the world. So old, in fact, that they still have solid bones. Their bones are heavy, compared to the featherweight hollow bones of most birds. They have small wings compared to their bodies, relative to other birds. Combine their weight and wing design, and you can imagine the size of the open water area that loons need for takeoff, sometimes as much as a quarter mile. It looks like loons run on the water before they become airborne. But once they lift off, they fly very fast. They've been clocked at speeds of up to ninety miles per hour. . . .

I felt guilty that I was getting paid to be a loon warden because I loved the job so much. My days involved leisurely cruises in a state-provided sixteen-foot boat to determine how many loons were nesting on the lake and where they were. Most of the nests were on small islands. My job was to watch the nests from shore with a powerful spotting scope and find out when the loons laid their eggs. I needed to know when those eggs were going to hatch because I had to make sure the nests were not disturbed while the eggs were hatching and when the chicks were newborn. . . .

Hanging out with the loons over the course of three seasons, it was amazing how intimate I became with them. I came to see that each had a personality. Some would be very nervous about any encroachment into their territory, especially from a motorboat. Others appeared quite serene. Because their legs are situated far back on their torso, loons can't walk. In fact, on land they push and pull themselves along with their feet and wings, bellies rubbing against the ground. Their awkwardness on land makes them vulnerable and skittish, to differing degrees. A boat might be one thousand feet away and a particular pair of loons will bolt from their nest into the water.

Another pair might tolerate a boat coming to an outrageous fifteen feet from their nest before they bolt.

A bolting loon is a hazard to its eggs—it can inadvertently drag them into the water. If that happens, the pair will not be able to get the eggs back into the nest. A bolting loon may also crush its eggs, which I saw happen more than once.

Part of my job was to protect the loons. People can easily end up loving loons to death. It's not that they want to hurt loons, but sometimes they don't know to keep far enough away. If someone comes too close to a nest, loons will see that as a threat. They may start to do a penguin dance, which looks like the loon is running on the water, flapping its wings, and tremoloing. This is an extremely photogenic fuss, and I've seen people come closer and closer to a loon's nest, shooting pictures, not understanding that the loon is telling them in no uncertain terms to please vacate its territory.

Sometimes my morning would start off with an incredibly flat mirror-like lake—so flat, so pristine, so virgin, so still that it felt like it would be a sacrilege to move through it. The silence was so intense that I hated to start up the motor. I was always in a hurry to stop the boat, stop the motor, stop the noise; to just be there in that incredible stillness, listening for a wail of a loon or the soft little hoots of geese in the distance. The silence and the mirror-like water seemed to say, "Stop. Do not enter. Sacred space." . . .

A pair of loons had nested in the Hop Brook area of Quabbin on a piece of land that changed with the reservoir's water level. In spring, when the water was high, it was a small island, and the loons nested on its outer part, out in the lake, close to a channel that separated their island from another island about fifty feet away.

When the water level dropped, the island became a peninsula. Raccoons could get out there, and two years in a row the coons had raided the loons' nest and eaten the eggs. There was also another danger to this nest. Between the two islands was a channel right next to the nest. The channel led to a small secluded cove, an excellent spot for fishing. Fishermen would drive their motorboats right through that little channel between the two islands, scaring the loons off the nest. The loons couldn't see the fishermen coming until the last minute, and then they would bolt off the nest.

During the spring and early summer of my third year on the job, I studied that nest long and hard. I felt particularly protective of these loons, and one day, I saw that there were eggs in the nest. I had a sense of foreboding, counting out the twenty-eight to thirty days of gestation. Sure enough, the eggs were due to hatch over the July Fourth weekend, Quabbin's busiest time.

I made sure that I was watching the nest on that weekend. It was an anxious, exciting time. For three consecutive years, I'd watched these loons establish their territory and build their nest. I'd watched them take turns sitting on their eggs, mouths agape, breathing hard to keep themselves cool in the hot sun. For two years they had failed to have chicks, and now the magic hour approached. Then I saw it: the smallest little thing emerged, about the size of a newly hatched baby chicken, all fuzzy and black. At first, all I saw was its tiny black head.

Only one loon was tending the nest when the chick hatched. I didn't know where the other loon was, and I didn't know whether it was the male or female on the nest. About three hours after the chick hatched, I saw a motorboat approaching the channel between the islands. I was horrified. I didn't want the loon to bolt off its nest and damage the newborn chick.

I jumped up and down on shore, waving at the boat. I don't know if they saw me. I ran out to the peninsula to try to warn the boat off. I was too late. The boat went through the channel quite fast. I motioned to the boat to approach me and explained the situation to the fishermen, who quickly motored away. I ran as fast as I could back to my spotting scope, breathless by the time I arrived.

I couldn't see the chick. The loon was in the water. It started to move slowly back to the nest. It acted strangely as it approached the nest. It kept putting its beak close to the area on the side of the nest where I had last seen the chick. It started to tremolo and wail, wail and tremolo. Finally, from across the water, I heard an answering wail. The other bird flew in.

One loon sat on the nest while the other swam back and forth in the cove. Both birds were agitated, tremoloing in unison. The bird on the nest put its beak close to where I had last seen the chick. It got on and off the nest several times. Both loons swam back and forth, tremoloing. The sound broke my heart. They actually took off together, which is rare, tremoloing, only to come back and take off again.

One of the last times that they took off, I ran to the nest. I had a strong suspicion of what I would find. There was the chick, limp and crushed. It had been run over when its parent bolted off the nest when the boat had come through the channel.

from THE WILD WITHIN

Message From a Hawk

ALLEN M. SCHOEN AND PAM PROCTOR

I knew it wasn't just an accident that brought me together with the hawk. He was a red-tail, a beautiful brownish bird of prey with a tuft of white feathers on his breast and a streak of red across his tail. At the time I met him, my career had taken me to New Paltz, New York, where I was working in a practice specializing in small animals and wildlife. The bird was brought into my office one morning by a passerby who had picked him up off the road. The man had watched in horror as the hawk flew into an electrical wire, then plunged to the ground.

Paralyzed from the neck down, the hawk couldn't lift a wing or even a claw. All the poor creature could do was move his head back and forth. I took the massive, eighteen-inch bird in my hands and looked him straight in the eye. He shot me a proud, piercing look that froze me in my place. With nothing but his cold, sharp eyes, he was trying to defend himself. Even though he was paralyzed and in my hands, he was telling me unequivocally, "Don't you touch me!"

Most human beings assume that a bird of prey is distant and dangerous—totally unapproachable. In this situation, I even found myself being judgmental. The hawk was so off-putting that I wondered if I could relate to this animal the same way I connected with dogs or cats.

Yet, without uttering a sound, he had spoken to me. He had demanded my respect, and I gave it to him instantly. I also gave him a name—Hawkeye—after the intrepid backwoods-man in James Fenimore Cooper's *The Last of the Mohicans.* The name summed up everything about my newest patient, a majestic hunter and king of his domain who claimed the right to live on *his* terms.

Right then and there, I committed myself to his recovery. I was his only link to life, and whether he wanted my help or not, I would give myself over to him until he regained his former glory.

I knew that for such an independent creature, rehabilitation could mean only one thing: to fly on his own, without a trace of disability. But it seemed like an impossible task. Helping to heal a pet was one thing. But a wild bird? A raptor that had once soared above the trees ready to swoop groundward for his day's kill? Could I ever hope to communicate with such a creature?

As I watched him eyeing me angrily from the examining table, I realized that if I had any chance of hearing his special voice, I would have to free myself of any preconceptions. I would have to use every ounce of my creativity and concern to penetrate through his paralysis and pride. I had to accept him as he was, listen for his cues, and proceed at his pace.

Over the next three months, for an hour or so a day, I devoted myself to bringing Hawkeye back to health. To feed him, I brought in "frozen dinners." Nearby, the Raptor Center at the State University at New Paltz had a ready store of frozen mice. I would defrost a mouse, cut it in pieces, and feed it to him bit by bit.

At first, whenever I approached Hawkeye's cage, he would

fix a beady eye on me and give me his cold, hard stare, as though he was contemplating an attack. Despite his defiance, I went about my business purposefully, feeding him the mice and keeping up a cheerful monologue about how good they tasted and how much energy they were giving him

His response was to gobble the food greedily—and then glare at me until I fed him some more. But day after day, as he came to understand that he was dependent on me for his food, he changed. Whenever I walked toward his cage, his defiance faded and a glow of acceptance seemed to shine from his eyes.

Along with the frozen dinners came his daily physical therapy. My technician and I took turns moving his wings, stretching his legs, and massaging his neck. My goal was to strengthen the muscles and increase circulation, just as he would do himself if he were able.

Through this constant physical attention over a period of weeks, such a bond grew between us that he would start screeching for me as soon as he heard the sound of my voice. As for me, when I heard him call, I quickened my pace toward the room with his cage. I would open the door, poke my head in, and with the joy of encountering a close friend, I would say gently, "Hello, Hawkeye, buddy. How're you doing?"

Only then did his screeching stop.

Slowly, ever so slowly, he started to come around. With each passing day, as I nursed him and fed him, the incredible possibilities of healing were unfolding right before my eyes. Against the odds, this independent, suspicious, wild creature that had been paralyzed and who would have been written off as a terminal case by the rest of the medical establishment began to improve.

After about three weeks of physical therapy, I decided

Hawkeye might be ready to try to walk. So I put him on the floor and waited. Tentatively, he took a step forward—but then he collapsed. I held him up as he again struggled to place one talon on the ground, and then the other.

He was still so weak that I had to massage him right then and there, carefully pulling and stretching his legs and claws. Several months later, I learned that I was unknowingly utilizing a form of acupressure or shiatsu—which is the art of massaging specific areas of the body used in acupuncture. But at the time, I was simply going on instinct in trying to exercise his body as best I could. Then, after a good massage, we went back to the task at hand—learning to walk. I would hold him up, he would put one foot in front of the other, and together we would "stroll" along the floor.

His condition improved daily. As soon as he was able to walk on his own, I decided why not go for broke? It was time to start getting him ready to fly. We had a large meshed-in aviary outside, which was perfect for our trial takeoffs. Like some medieval lord, I put a leather gauntlet on my arm and attached long leather straps to the hawk.

Hawkeye clutched my arm with his talons and started flapping his wings. The flutter of those once-inert wings sent a thrill through me, and I remembered how as a ten-year-old I had raised a baby starling and taught him to fly. His claws would grip my finger, and as I raised my arm up and down, he flapped his wings until he was ready, at last, to take off.

Now, on a much more dramatic scale, I was doing a similar thing with Hawkeye. I moved my arm up and down, and, like the starling, the hawk flapped his wings harder and harder to keep from falling. He clung to my arm for a few days, then he bravely took off—and immediately headed straight down!

I cringed in pain as he landed with a thud at my feet.

But Hawkeye didn't give up. He looked at me, and with eyes that were at once imploring and determined, he seemed to say, "I *must* keep going."

With that, I put him back on my arm and we tried again. He kept leaping and falling again until finally, a few days later, he managed to fly two feet before falling.

Then one day I released the straps and he flew up to one of the beams that were arranged like branches at the top of the aviary. He would hop along the beam and then fly to another one, slowly testing his newfound strength. Eventually, he was able to fly around the entire aviary. For hours he would fly back and forth, gripping the wire mesh on the sides, as though begging to be released outside.

Finally, when he seemed fully healed, I let him go outside the aviary. He took off from my arm and circled around and around overhead, as though clinging to invisible tethers. Perhaps it was his way of holding on as long as he could to his now familiar world of frozen mice and human friendship. For a week or two, he hung around outside, staying in the trees and screeching when he wanted his food.

Then, one day, he disappeared. Just like that. I stood searching the treetops, longing for some glimpse of him, but I knew he was gone forever. My emotions warred between pride and sorrow. I had poured out myself to help heal this hawk, and now he had abandoned me. I felt like a father who had sent his son on some far-off adventure that could not be shared.

But I wasn't left empty-handed. In his place, Hawkeye had given me a precious gift that propelled me on an incredible adventure of my own. By a stroke of fate, a charged electrical wire, I had been afforded the privilege of penetrating the inner world of a wild, rapacious creature, an animal that was born to kill.

From the beginning Hawkeye had set the pace. Instinctively he had thrown up a wall of hostility to protect himself from harm. But as I had patiently and humbly cared for him and listened attentively to the signals he gave me, he had dropped his guard and revealed to me his courage, his determination, and his capacity to care.

Hawkeye had given me a window on what may be nature's greatest secret: that no creature can remain forever closed to the healing power of love. I knew that if I could establish an intimate relationship with a bird of prey, I could communicate with *any* animal, no matter how distant or fearsome it might appear to be. All I would need was a sensitivity of spirit, a willingness to open myself nonjudgmentally to a dimension of reality where feathers, fur, skin, scales, or hair are stripped away—and where the only language is love.

Hawkeye had his freedom, and now I had mine. He had given me my wings, and I was ready to soar.

from LOVE, MIRACLES, AND ANIMAL HEALING

Winged Spirit

JEANNE B. FLETCHER

$\mathcal{A}$lthough I love birds in general, the mockingbird has to be my all-time favorite. This sassy, feisty little creature has given me so many hours of pleasure from the beautiful nighttime songs during nesting to the foolhardy but comical bravery displayed when their territory is threatened. I've seen mockingbirds chase dogs, cats, and even people who venture too near their homestead, swooping and diving and refusing to give up while the intruder was still too close. They are smart and aggressive, but friendly.

For 30 years I have been able to call mockingbirds to my kitchen door with a little tick-ticking sound. They know they'll get raisins and grapes when they respond, and they quickly learn that I am a friend. If I don't call them first, they will call to me from the tree outside the door—mimicking the sound I make.

When my oldest daughter, Jennifer, who was affectionately nicknamed Jenny Wren from the nursery rhymes, was six, I sent for a book called *Hand-Taming Wild Birds at the Feeder.* I already had a friendly mockingbird who would sit on the patio outside the French doors until I tossed her some raisins, and this was the bird I wanted to hand-tame.

I started by sitting in a lawn chair on the patio and calling the bird, who came readily. I tossed the raisins on the grass, and she didn't hesitate for a moment in snatching them up. I followed by dropping the raisins near my chair on the patio. A little cagey at first, watching me constantly as I sat very still, she then approached and took the treats. Over the next two days, I put the raisins on a tray table right next to my chair, and she had to land on the table. I think that was the hardest step for her. She had to come so near to my hand, and it took quite a few minutes before her instinctive courage and desire for the raisins overcame her nervousness. After that, it was so easy that I couldn't believe it.

Next, I put my hand on the table with the raisins in my open palm, and she plucked them right off. Then, the big test. I held up my hand with the raisins and called to my friend. She flew around a bit, then landed on my outstretched hand and took her raisins. I was delighted, and I think my mockingbird was just as pleased.

When Jenny wanted to try it, I instructed her to stay very still and not wave her hand around. She called the bird, and what a thrill it was for her when that little bundle of feathers landed on her small hand and took the fruit. Jenny never forgot it, and she always loved birds.

Some years later, when Jenny was a registered nurse, we teased her about being a "bird nurse" because she resuscitated a robin and a starling that had flown into the window and knocked themselves senseless. When Jenny heard the robin crack against the window, she rushed outside to find him lying still with his beak open but unable to draw a breath. She picked him up and blew gently into his beak. Within minutes the robin recovered and flew off. The same thing happened with the starling.

In the spring of 1989, when our Jenny Wren had turned 26, she was diagnosed with inoperable cancer, and on a fine April morning, just less than a year later, she died at home, which was her wish. I was holding her hand when she left and wondering how such a small hand had enough stretch to play the piano so beautifully. I remembered how the mockingbird ate from it 20 years before . . . and how excited she had been. She had such zest for life, and she hadn't wanted to be isolated from the family, so we had a bed for her in the rec room, which opens directly from the kitchen. She could see the trees and hear the birds singing, with the activity of her family and her German shepherd all around her.

Shortly after she died, while we were awaiting the funeral director, I heard a rustling sound from the living room. I went to investigate, and it was the strangest moment I can recall. A tiny bird had gotten into the house through the dog access. As I opened the doors and gently ushered the bird to freedom, I saw it was a wren. It was like a message from Jenny that even though she had to leave, she was still with us.

I later discovered that the wren had built a nest in the cooler hung on the wall outside. When the wren returned the following spring, I was happy to see her. She seemed to be a symbol of rebirth and resurrection, and the comfort of knowing that our own Jenny Wren would always be with us in spirit and in our hearts.

from HEART SONGS FOR ANIMAL LOVERS

A Bell for Rajah

JOHN K. TERRES

I still remember the bright spring day when I found my first turkey vulture nest. I was eleven years old and living in a village in southern New Jersey. I had walked several miles from my home at the edge of town, as I did almost every day, to explore an oak forest, a creek, and a marsh.

As I neared the top of the wooded slope, I saw in a clearing a large hollow log. Suddenly a vulture ran out of it and flapped into the air. I stood startled, not knowing whether to run or stay. I had always been fearful of vultures, and I was relieved when the bird glided away. Scared as I was, however, I had to know what was inside that log. I ran to it, peeped in, then crawled within. In the dim light, on the rotting bottom, I saw two large white eggs.

When I returned a week later, the eggs had hatched and two small downy white vultures sat clumsily on the floor of the log. I crawled to them and picked them up as I would baby chicks in our poultry house at home. I stroked them for a while, running my fingers over their homely heads and sharply hooked bills. Their eyes were open and they made no protest at my handling of them, other than a low hiss. They gave off no odor. The smaller one seemed so helpless that I could not bear to leave him. I left the larger one in the log but took the smaller one home.

That was the way Rajah came into my life. I called him Rajah because, even when he was very young, he held his black-skinned head high and had a defiant way of sitting back proudly on his haunches and hissing fiercely when I tried to pick him up. Later, when I learned Rajah's language—I never heard him make a sound other than a hiss—I knew what he meant simply by noting how softly or loudly he hissed. A low hiss, which he always gave when I was feeding him, meant he was pleased; a loud vigorous one, that he was angry.

Everyone in the village soon knew that I had a vulture. It was unthinkable to many people—*no one* had ever kept a *vulture* as a pet. Men, and some boys of my own age, came to our yard to stare at my big white chick and to remark sarcastically that anyone must be crazy to want a stinking vulture for a pet.

I defended Rajah—he had no odor, at least not at that time. Besides, I had always pitied turkey vultures. Life seemed so difficult for them—they were always gliding about searching for food. It seemed to me that any bird that had to wait for another animal to die might, on occasion, have to wait a long time.

The soaring flight of the turkey vulture, or buzzard as it was called locally, was the most graceful of any bird I had ever seen. Yet everyone in my village spoke of vultures contemptuously, or in disgust—they were scavengers that fed on the putrefying flesh of other animals. Vultures seemed to be doomed as outcasts from other birds, too. They were always on the fringe of bird society, never associating with others, except with their own kind.

Farmers and hunters, in their ignorance and prejudice, often shot and killed vultures simply because they thought they were ugly, and because they made easy targets. Naked-headed and hunched, they sat about on fenceposts or in trees not far from the carcass of some animal, awaiting their turn to feed. No one spoke of them as a sanitation corps—that they were performing a useful health service to the community in cleaning up the carcasses of the dead animals and helping to prevent the spread of dreaded anthrax and cholera. My schoolteacher had told me that. I knew also that, someday, these people who hated vultures might even kill Rajah.

But at the moment I had a more urgent worry than the disapproval of the villagers. I did not know what to feed Rajah, or where I might safely keep him. My mother did not want me to have Rajah, and much as she liked birds, she did not want a vulture in the house. I decided to keep him in the poultry yard—if the chickens would accept him.

Rajah was almost as large as some of the hens themselves, and when I first released him, they pecked at him and tried to chase him away. But Rajah hissed loudly, spread his wings, and struck back with his sharply hooked bill. Immediately this established Rajah right at the top of the peck order in the henyard. However, it was to be different when the "silver-lace" Wyandotte rooster came. But that was much later, and the one-eyed monster we called "Long John Silver" had every right by his poultry-yard standards to do what he did to Rajah. Long John had lost his right eye in a fight with another Wyandotte, but that did not stop him from fighting if he was challenged.

Although Rajah did not trust dogs, he tolerated our small water spaniel, whose long silky coat was as black as Rajah's adult feathers would be. But if a strange dog came into the yard, Rajah would hiss loudly, then attack it with a furious flailing of his strong wings, black beak, and claws. Perhaps, in the dim recesses of his vulture mind, he associated the shape or color of certain dogs with that of foxes. Hunters said that if a fox den were located near the nest of a turkey vulture, which is usually on the ground in a woodland, a rock cave, or simply on the floor of the swamp, the foxes might kill the young vultures and eat them, or carry them off to feed them to their own young.

I almost lost my vulture the first week I had him. I tried to feed Rajah raw meat scraps, but he merely sat back and eyed them and made no attempt to pick them up, nor would he take them from my fingers. He also refused to drink milk or water from a bowl I set before him. By the third day he began to crouch flat on the ground in his hunger and weakness. I did not dare tell my mother that Rajah would not eat. That would have been to admit defeat, and she would have made me return Rajah at once to his nesting log.

That first Sunday after I had taken Rajah from the nest, while my mother was at church, my uncle who lived on a farm nearby dropped in to see me. I think he had heard about the vulture. He loved animals and had kept many wild pets of his own. When he saw Rajah his usually laughing face went grave.

"He's starving," he said, and he looked at me angrily.

"I don't know what to feed him," I said helplessly.

"Vultures eat dead animals, don't they?" he asked. I nodded.

"Well, we've got to give him something that a young vulture will eat, and I think I know what it should be."

We went into the house and my uncle opened our old-fashioned refrigerator. He brought out the remains of a cooked chicken we had for dinner that day. Crumbling the meat into bits with his strong fingers, he mixed it in a bowl with some rich gravy. When he had finished we went into the yard and he set the bowl in front of Rajah. But the vulture only looked up at us helplessly. I was ready to cry. Then I had a sudden thought.

"He's always putting his bill into my partly closed hands,"

I said. "Mr. Daniels at the grocery store says this might be a sign he wants to eat out of my hand."

My uncle smacked his big palms together as though I had made a great discovery. His blue eyes were warm again. "Boy," he said, "I think you've got it! Go into the house and get me that tin cup you drink out of." I ran and got it and handed it to him. With a blow of his big fist my uncle flattened it. Then he poured the soupy chicken gravy and ground meat into the cup and held it before Rajah. Rajah shoved his bill into it, and when my uncle tilted the cup toward him, Rajah began to feed. His bill and tongue made soft noises as he fed.

I never knew until years later why Rajah had refused raw meat yet was so quick to drink from the tin cup. In the beginning, a young vulture does not eat solid food. It takes soft food, regurgitated by the parent, from inside the old bird's bill. Our flattened cup, a receptacle that resembled the shape of a vulture's bill, had elicited an instant instinctive response from Rajah. I think that my uncle, shrewd in the ways of wild things, knew this, or had guessed it. But he let me believe that he had saved Rajah only with my help and with a big piece of luck from a rabbit's left hind foot that I always carried in my left hind pocket.

After that, feeding Rajah was no problem. Besides meat gravy, he even drank milk and water from the cup. One day he surprised me when he began to feed himself by catching lizards that ran across our yard and big grasshoppers that flew up in front of him from the sandy road by our house. I had always been told that vultures ate only dead animals, but Rajah was proving me wrong about his kind. One hot July day I was horrified to see Rajah pounce on a three-foot-long black snake that glided across our lawn. He swallowed it slowly with convulsive gulps, then looked at me in a way that I recognized as his "hungry look." His appetite was improving.

As Rajah grew stronger, his black feathers began to replace his soft babyish down. Each day he tried to fly. At least he *seemed* to be trying to fly as he stood on our lawn flapping his long black wings. But like a plane revving its motors, Rajah was only warming up for future flights because in his practice he never got off the ground.

It was not until August that he began to lift himself into the air, and with his new ability I began to worry again. Someday I might lose him. Later I learned that it takes about a month for a young turkey vulture to hatch and another two and a half months before it can fly.

Now Rajah's efforts began to show progress. He would run across the lawn beating his wings wildly, and he succeeded several times in bounding a couple of feet into the air. One day he practiced so enthusiastically that he almost came to disaster. Flapping his wings and leaping ahead, he crashed into one of my mother's wooden clothes posts that supported the washline. He collapsed and lay there all in a heap, but he was only stunned by the impact and soon recovered.

Each night, after shutting the chickens in the henhouse, I put Rajah inside the adjoining fenced poultry yard where a night-roving fox or raccoon could not get him. Although he was safe inside the pen, I was afraid that one morning before I got up Rajah might take off and I would never see him again. Had I known of the late-rising habits of wild vultures, perhaps I would not have been so concerned.

Before Rajah could fly, I knew that I had to mark him in some way so I could recognize him if he came back, soaring over our house, a wild free bird. Just a leg band or something of that sort would not do. I thought he should announce his return like the town criers of old. I had an idea.

One day I tucked the big vulture under an arm and carried him to the village harness shop. There, while I held Rajah, the harness-maker carefully fitted Rajah's black-feathered neck with a neatly fitting leather strap. Now all I needed was a bell. Somewhere I had heard of a belled vulture, and the idea appealed to me enormously. Rajah, carrying his swinging neck bell, would be as easy for me to distinguish as a flying falcon that is recognized by her master from the tinkling of her leg bells.

I boarded a country streetcar, and three miles away in a small neighboring city I found what I wanted. It was a small, lightweight dinner bell, displayed in the window of a hardware store. When I held it in my hands and shook it, it had the loveliest sound of any bell I had ever heard.

Back in my yard, I caught Rajah, held him under one arm, and tried to fasten the bell to his leather collar with a piece of wire. Rajah was big and strong, and he squirmed and tried to beat his wings. I had carefully pinned them to his sides, but I had forgotten about his sharp claws. Before I finally fastened the bell to the strap, one of my arms was bleeding from the raking of Rajah's claws in his struggles to get free. But Rajah had his bell, and I knew that if he did fly away, I would be able to recognize him if he ever came back.

One afternoon in September, when I came home from school, Rajah was gone. I didn't know how or when he had gotten into the air, but presumably one of Rajah's takeoffs had been successful. I was sorry I had not been there to see it, and I worried for fear he would never come back.

The next day, when I came home for lunch, I heard Rajah's bell tinkling. He was sitting on one of the tall posts of the poultry yard, and by the way he craned his neck eagerly toward me, I knew he was hungry. He flew to the ground and waddled to the tin cup I held toward him. I had filled it with his favorite meat and gravy. When he came near, however, I got a shock. The odor that came from Rajah was rich, overripe, and nauseating. Somewhere out in the fields or woods he had fed on the dead carcass of some animal, perhaps in company with other vultures.

I held my nose with one hand while Rajah fed from the cup that I held in the other. When he had eaten his fill, Rajah turned away. He ran across the lawn, flapping his wings heavily as he went, then rose into the air. He circled the house once, his bell tinkling faintly, then soared out over a field. As he spiraled upward, he moved away with a strong wind that carried him far out over the pine forest the villagers called "Horse Heaven." It was a remote place where the village sanitation wagon dumped dead horses and other animals to be disposed of by the vultures.

By now I was familiar with an ancient village argument: Did the turkey buzzards that filled the skies over Horse Heaven at the dumping of each newly dead animal find them by their sharp eyesight, or by their sense of smell? There were heated claims by hunters and fishermen who took opposing sides, but I was unable to help settle it. Rajah had never shown me exactly how he knew I had food for him, even when I hid it behind me in the tin cup. If I stood before him without food, he stared at me accusingly out of his black eyes, but if I did have the cup with the mixture in it, even though I kept it hidden under my jacket, Rajah rushed excitedly around me. He *knew* that I had the food hidden on my person. I always suspected that he smelled the concoction, although I was not sure.

Rajah did not come back, and about a week after he had gone we got Long John Silver, the Wyandotte rooster. My father said the rooster would protect hens from attacks by hawks. A few days later, a Cooper's hawk swooped into the poultry yard and tried to seize a hen. Now Long John proved his worth. He leaped high in the air, his spurred feet thrust out at the hawk. Repelled by the fury of the rooster's attack, the hawk flew rapidly away. Now Long John *knew* he was the cock of the walk, and his one-eyed fury was directed even toward me if I came too close to the pen.

It was a week later that Rajah came back. I had eaten my lunch and was out on the lawn when I heard the tinkle of his bell. He soared over the yard, dropping lower and lower. Then he glided down and alighted in the poultry yard. Rajah was used to the hens, but now he got the shock of his young life. At that moment, Long John Silver dashed straight at Rajah. The fury of the rooster's attack almost knocked Rajah over, but he quickly recovered.

I will say this—Rajah was no coward. Although out-weighed by five pounds, he raised his six-foot spread of wings and rushed at Long John. He struck at the rooster with his hooked bill, but the eight-pound Wyandotte, besides being heavier, was much too agile for the three-pound vulture.

The rooster clinched savagely with Rajah, pulling out some of his feathers and striking him with spurred feet. The vulture turned away, ran a few steps, and with a silky rustling of his wings lifted into the air. Long John, possibly stunned for a moment by the size of his foe rising above him, paused. In that instant, Rajah left the chicken yard and swung upward and out-ward, his bell tinkling, his black wings beating heavily on the air. He soared far across a field, turned into the wind, and circled up and up until he was a black speck in the sky. Then he drifted southward and disappeared below the blue horizon.

I never saw Rajah again. After I moved away, some of the hunters and fishermen of the village told my uncle that they heard a bell tinkling in the skies the following spring.

I could not forget Rajah, nor did I want to. He had become a living example of his kind, and of the cruelties inflicted by the blindly prejudiced on the misunderstood. Rajah had been my first wild pet, and he had been the first to teach me that language is not necessary to understanding. Like all wild animals I have ever known, Rajah had a way of communicating that was distinctly and very beautifully all his own.

from THE AUDUBON WILDLIFE TREASURY

Wild Things Must Be Free

PHYLLIS HOBE

$\mathcal{I}$ live next to a waterfowl sanctuary in southeastern Pennsylvania, and every spring birds come to nest and breed in the fields surrounding a lake I can see from my house. One day last spring I looked out my kitchen window and saw a flight of Canada geese approaching in their familiar V formation. As I reached for my binoculars I heard three gun blasts. I was furious. Hunting isn't permitted in the sanctuary.

At first the birds seemed to stagger in the air, and then they continued their flight. *They're all right,* I thought. But a moment later, I saw a large Canada goose in my backyard. It was limping toward the fields, dragging its left wing. I could see some blood on it.

Immediately I thought of my friend Mary Jane Stretch. She is a wildlife rehabilitator, a rather technical title for someone who knows how to help wild creatures when they're in trouble. Each year she treats thousands of injured animals at the Aark Foundation, a shelter she founded almost 20 years ago. Most of her patients are released back into the wild.

"Mary Jane, I don't even know how to pick up a goose!" I told her when I explained what had happened.

"Take a towel and throw it over the head," she said. "But be careful how you handle it—that long neck has a lot of striking power." She told me how to place one hand under the goose's bill, to control its neck. "Then just wrap your arms around its body and pick it up."

When I went out in the fields the goose was still struggling toward the lake. I felt very clumsy next to it. The poor bird trembled in fright as I threw the towel and missed. On my third attempt the towel wafted down over the bird's head.

I picked up the goose and held it against me. It struggled for a moment, then relaxed as if it had no choice but to trust me. Touched by its helplessness, I began to cry. What a beautiful creature it was, its head and neck a soft shade of black and its body pewter-gray. I marveled at the texture and thickness of its feathers: They felt like velvet. "Don't worry, I won't hurt you," I kept whispering.

In my garage I found an old box. I put the goose in and draped a towel over the top, then I put the box on the backseat of my car and set off for the Aark. During the hour-long drive the goose didn't make a sound. I began to worry about the silence. "Please, Lord, don't let it die." To my relief I heard it stirring.

As I parked in front of the Aark, Mary Jane's daughter Samantha came out to help me. As soon as I turned off the engine the goose was out of the box and flapping its wings desperately in the backseat. With a sweep of her arms Sammy deftly enveloped the bird and carried it into the intensive care unit in the barn.

"Fortunately the shot went through the wing and broke only a few small bones," Mary Jane said after she examined the goose.

She began to prepare an antibiotic. "So far, it looks good, but there may be some damage I haven't found."

"What'll you do with it if it gets better?" I asked. I had been thinking the goose might make a nice pet.

"We'll turn it loose," Mary Jane said.

"Where?" I wanted to know. I was beginning to speak as if the goose belonged to me.

"Some place where it can be with other geese," she said.

During the next weeks I called Mary Jane almost every day to find out about "my" goose. She had put it outside in a flight pen, which allowed it enough space to fly, but the goose wasn't making any effort to get off the ground. "It's been hurt," Mary Jane explained. "It lost contact with its flock, its mate. But I think this goose will fly again."

"Do we have to let it go?" I said. "Couldn't I keep it? I'll take good care of it."

"I know you would," Mary Jane said gently. "But there are laws against keeping wildlife, and for good reasons. Wild things aren't like your dog and cat, Phyllis. They aren't meant to live in our world."

I wasn't entirely convinced and Mary Jane sensed it. "I have an idea," she said. "When we release this goose, would you come with us?"

"Oh, yes!" I said excitedly. Then almost immediately, I felt sad. How would I feel watching this lovely bird go back to an existence so filled with danger? I wanted to protect it, not only from animal predators, but from human ones as well.

I continued to feel ambivalent, but the time came when the goose could fly. One sunny morning Mary Jane called to say she was going to release it that afternoon along with a mallard duck. She told me to meet her at Lake Galena in a county park about halfway between our houses. "It's a lovely area for water-fowl," she said.

I met Mary Jane and her assistant, Diane Nickerson, at a parking area overlooking a lake that seemed to stretch for miles. The sun was low on the horizon; among the greenery were the delicate white and pink blossoms of wild cherry trees and dogwood. Far to our left we could see geese out on the water, and to our right, ducks. Looking directly across the lake, I caught my breath. There in perfect profile was an enormous white swan.

We inched down the bank to the water, Mary Jane with the mallard in her arms, Diane carrying the big box with the Canada goose in it.

The mallard was the first to be released. Mary Jane lowered it into the water, and it swam straight out in the direction of the swan, its brilliant emerald-green head like a jewel in the sun. To my disappointment the duck never even looked back.

"Once they're well, wild things don't really want to stay with people," Mary Jane said, reading the expression on my face.

Now Mary Jane lifted the goose out of the box. Its long neck arched back and swept forward suddenly, but Mary Jane ducked just in time as the bird pulled its wings free of her grasp. The moment it felt the water under its body, the goose glided out toward the swan. Not even a glance back.

"That's good," Diane said. "We don't want them to get friendly with people. In their world it isn't safe."

Watching both birds getting smaller and smaller, I was happy for them, but sorry to see them leave. "You must feel this way often," I said to Mary Jane and Diane.

"It's part of helping them," Mary Jane said. "The best part—getting them healthy enough to go back where they belong. But you can't help wanting to hold on to them too." She began climbing up the hill, and when she reached the top she looked back at the lake. The duck, the goose and the swan were going their separate ways.

"Wild things have to be free," she said. "That's the way God made them."

In the Waters

*"The face of the sea is as variable
as that of the earth."*

ANTOINE DE SAINT EXUPERY

It's hard for us to believe that earth's waters are home to so many of God's creatures. But stand on the end of a pier and look down for a while, and you will begin to see how much life goes on there. Go out in a boat and, instead of fishing, just watch. Stand along a sandy shore as the waves roll in and be amazed at the life that swirls around your feet.

Like the land and the sky, the waters are part of our world. So are the animals God created to live here.

The Newborn Whale

EDITH THACHER HURD

On the flat blue sea there were only the white fountains of the whales.

The mother sperm whale rocked in the long slow waves of the sea, waiting.

The great bull whale swam around and around. The bottle-nosed dolphins dove in the blue sea and leaped in the sunshine.

At last it was time. The mother whale held herself still, her tail moved back and forth. She balanced herself with her flippers. For one year and four months the baby whale had been curled up and growing. It was now time for it to be born.

The baby whale was born slowly, first his tail, the two black flukes curled in at the corners, just as they had been while he was growing inside his mother. Last of all came the baby whale's flippers and his huge head. He was a big baby. He weighed two thousand pounds and was fourteen feet long.

The mother whale turned quickly. She pushed her new baby. She pushed him up, up—up to the fresh air above. The baby whale breathed his first breath. He breathed in big gulps of the new fresh air. Out through his blowhole, he breathed small white spurts of air and water.

The mother whale grunted and made singing noises as she swam close to her little new calf. He moved his tail slowly and balanced himself with his flippers. He shivered in the cold ocean water.

The bull whale swam not too close but not far away. The beautiful dolphins leaped together in the sunshine, and no hungry sharks or fast-swimming killer whales came near the baby.

The mother whale turned on her side. Her baby nuzzled her belly. He drank her warm milk, gallons and gallons and gallons of warm rich milk.

Then the baby whale lay still, floating in the slow waves that washed over him. Birds flew over him, screaming. But the baby whale did not hear them. He was sleeping.

from THE MOTHER WHALE

Three Gray Whales

JEAN CRAIGHEAD GEORGE

For twenty-one days three gray whales fought for life and breath in the frozen Beaufort Sea, while television viewers around the world watched them in pain and hope.

Bone, Bonnet and Crossbeak, three endangered California gray whales, had left the Arctic Ocean at the end of summer and were on their way to Baja California, Mexico, to breed and winter. Feeding close to shore at Point Barrow, Alaska, they lingered too long and were surrounded by ice on October 7, 1988. That evening an Eskimo hunter found the air-breathing sea mammals about two hundred yards from shore, struggling for breath in an opening in the ice.

He reported the plight of the whales to the biologists at the North Slope Borough Wildlife Management Department in Barrow. Both Eskimo and white scientists thought perhaps the whales should be put out of their misery. Then television got hold of the story and they wondered no more. Letters and phone calls poured in. The world wanted the three gray whales rescued.

Eskimo hunters together with the scientists set out to do so. Using chain saws, they cut a series of breathing holes leading toward open water three miles away. When this effort was shown on television, six-foot chain saws were sent to the rescuers by concerned businesspeople. . . . The rescuers went on sawing. As the days grew colder, the holes refroze. At their own expense, several people hopped a plane and arrived in Barrow with costly de-icing equipment.

The de-icers kept the water open for the whales, and the rescuers sawed on. Then something went wrong. The whales stopped using the holes. . . .

Then Malek, an elderly Eskimo hunter, spoke to the whales. After a while he reported to the rescuers: "The water is too shallow, the whales are saying." The scientists took a sounding of the lagoon bottom and found that the whales were right. A shoal was blocking the escape route. The water was too shallow under the breathing holes.

Urgently the men cut holes leading around the shoal, and urgently the whales responded. They swam from one hole to the next in great excitement as they moved toward the open sea.

On the eighteenth day of the rescue attempt, the holes stretched one and a half miles toward freedom, but the whales were growing weary. Bone, the smallest, disappeared and was never seen again.

That night a wind moved great floes of ice toward Point Barrow and piled them in a ridge twenty feet high. It grounded the ridge on the bottom of the lagoon and cut off all escape. The next morning, when Bonnet and Crossbeak were surfacing to breathe, Malek again went to the whales. . . . Day and night he remained with the gray whales, soothing them with his voice and stroking their ice-torn noses with his hands. . . .

Meanwhile around the world, television watchers turned on their sets each morning to see if the whales were still alive. At the White House's direction, the Air Force assigned a C-5A

Galaxy to ferry more equipment to Barrow. The President of the United States wished the whales well.

Then the Soviet Union responded. The cold-war enemy of the United States announced that two Soviet icebreakers three hundred miles from Barrow were on their way to help the whales.

Encouraged, the American rescuers sawed furiously forward, trying to reach the ridge in time to meet the Soviet icebreakers. Again the whales stopped swimming. This time the men knew why—shallow water. Since they were about five hundred feet from the ridge, they cut a big pool for the whales and went back to town to sleep and to wait for the Soviets—all but Malek. He stayed with the whales all night, stroking and calming them.

In the darkness of the morning of October 26, the rescue crew returned to watch the Soviet icebreakers cut a path through the ridge as if it were butter. The whales bolted for open water. Cheers went up, and it was reported that the whales were free.

They were not. They could not surface to breathe in the ice-jammed track. They came back to the last hole. Once more the Soviets cut through the ice. The whales moved but went the wrong way. They returned to the hole and thrust their heads above water. Malek talked to them, pointed them in the right direction and gave them a shove. With that, Bonnet and Crossbeak rose halfway out of the water in a breach, dove and disappeared.

The Soviet captain saw one pass his ship. At last the whales were free.

from ANIMALS WHO HAVE WON OUR HEARTS

Turtle By Moonlight

ELEANOR SASS

---

7 do enjoy unusual vacations. So, when I was invited to spend two weeks studying the migratory habits of turtles at a remote station in the Caribbean, I accepted. But, now that I was sitting all alone on a darkened beach in Costa Rica, I had misgivings. *Did I really care all that much about turtles?*

Then, in the bright moonlight, I saw a huge green turtle coming in with the breakers, rising with a wave, then bumping back softly on the sand. She peered into the night, as if making up her mind. Then, slowly but doggedly she made her way to the beach vegetation. I watched, mesmerized, as, flinging sand in every direction, she used her long front flippers to dig a pit for her body. With one of her rear flippers, she dug out an egg chamber. Soon she began to give great heaves, and the chamber filled with a hundred eggs, each about the size of a golfball.

After a while, she stopped and seemed to be resting. Then her front flippers started up again as she covered the pit with sand to conceal it from predators. Finally, her mission accomplished, she turned and headed back to the sea.

I watched as she disappeared. *Dear God, how endearing she is,* I thought. *And how uncanny her ability to find her natal beach, so she, in turn, can continue her species.*

As I trudged back to the station, I said a prayer for the safety of the turtle hatchlings who would emerge from the shells in about sixty days. *God's creatures. He cares about them. And He wants me to care about them, too.*

A Secret Place

JIM ARNOSKY

The snapping turtle clambered over the stubs of last year's corn, passing row after row before finding a spot that suited her. Then, turning and facing her own trail from the pond, she began making a nest hole in the soft spring soil. When she had dug as deep as her hind legs could reach, she began to lay her eggs. Each egg was pure white and as round as a Ping-Pong ball. They appeared one at a time, like doves from a magician's coat. Each was guided carefully into the sandy hole by the turtle's hind feet. After the last egg rolled gently into the nest, she buried the batch by pushing dirt over them with her body. She smoothed the spot with her bottom shell, then followed her tracks back to the water.

I stared at the spot of freshly worked earth and thought of the baby turtles that would develop and hatch there in sun-warmed ground. I looked to the pond and wondered if the snapping turtle had already forgotten her hidden eggs in the cornfield, because, if she had, the secret was all mine.

from SECRETS OF A WILDLIFE WATCHER

In the Presence of Dolphins

TONI G. FROHOFF

$\mathcal{I}$ have laughed underwater many times while swimming in the company of free-ranging dolphins. It's the type of laughter that erupts from my heart. And I have been met with the same shining eye by my dolphin companions as I have during my finest moments of friendship.

As I swim I am surrounded by dolphins—above me, below me, to either side. While some exchange places as they swim, others remain nearby, maintaining eye contact. "I am lost again as I am waking . . . " This phrase, written by Jim Carroll, keeps running through my mind as I recall the feeling of being in the midst of dolphins. The experience is surreal, yet my senses are more alive than ever. The dolphins' bodies around me feel somewhat protective, almost like a huge, flowing hand, supporting and guiding me gently. Their vocalizations come from every direction and I sometimes feel them on and inside of my body as their echolocation explores me. As I swim along, young dolphins occasionally dart in and out of our group, eyeing me most directly as they swim by. Their carefree exuberance is contagious and I know that I am in bliss.

I do not look forward as I swim. I feel safe in the presence of these exquisitely beautiful animals. But am I? As I swim up to the surface to take a breath of air, I look up and find myself staring straight ahead into a living wall of very large barracudas. I wonder why the dolphins have escorted me here. If I were to carefully construct a practical (or cosmic) joke, I could not have done it better myself. At this time in my life, I am unusually nervous when encountering even lone barracudas, who in these parts are very curious.

As I begin to initiate my panicky retreat, my instinct to flee is interrupted. I look around and see that several of the dolphins are still around me; they have remained at my side. They do not appear nervous at all and the barracudas do not seem particularly interested in any of us. Soon, calmed, I swim back toward our boat with my dolphin escorts. This experience has helped me ever since, when studying marine life in the company of extraordinarily curious or large barracudas and sharks. It was my first lesson in relying on the behavior of "predatory" animals rather than their reputation in determining my safety in their presence. I feel as if I was given a great gift—taught an invaluable lesson.

from BEYOND SPECIES (INTIMATE NATURE)

A Shark in Trouble

DON C. REED

You can imagine how I felt earlier that night when I was called at home and told that a net-caught white shark was being brought to Marine World. As head diver, I was naturally expected to help with the shark, meaning to get into the water with it. San Francisco's world-renowned Steinhart Aquarium had had the shark first, but their largest tank was not yet completed, and they had no enclosure big enough to house this diver's nightmare.

The ride to Marine World was the most terrifying forty minutes of my life. My stomach felt squeezed and kneaded by invisible fingers. The sky was black and seemed to be closing over my head. I envisioned every horrific possibility, remembered every shark attack scene I had ever read about or seen at the movies, imagined the teeth like knives, closing through my body. Maybe the shark would bite my swim fins off, with my feet still in them. I wished I were a kid again so I could go back to bed and forget the whole thing.

The animal waiting for me was small, as white sharks go, seven feet six inches, three hundred fifty pounds, but that gave me no comfort. The worst single shark attack in history, the real-life incident on which the book and movie *Jaws* were based, had involved a white shark only six inches longer. That had happened in 1916 at Matawan Creek, New Jersey. In a freak occurrence an eight-foot white shark had swum up a river and gotten trapped. Perhaps through fear or because it was denied its natural food, the white shark killed four people and wounded a fifth before it was caught and positively identified by the human remains in its stomach. "Our" shark from Steinhart was just about that size. What if it panicked, or got angry, thinking we were trying to hurt it?

All too quickly the distance passed, and I pulled up at the back gate of Marine World/Africa USA.

The guard shack was brightly lit, but when I'd run past the giraffe and elephant barns, past the shining eyes of wolves, and got to the divers' shower room, I had to dress in the dark. Redwood City was having some minor electrical supply problems that summer. That was okay, though. I was the largest diver and could pick out my wet suit by its weight. I stripped and climbed into the sleeveless "farmer johns," not bothering with the jacket this warm summer night. I was anxious to get into the water with the shark and not have to think about it anymore. When I was halfway suited up, the electricity came back on, which was a relief.

With swim fins and scuba gear and air hose on, I stood at the darkened staircase leading down to the entryway into the reef aquarium tank. The square of water below me *glowed*— a ghastly writhing green. It was only because floodlights had been set up to shine into the tank from the windowed hallway below, but knowing that did not help. To me right then, the wavering green water looked like the doorway to hell.

But, I reminded myself, the white shark from Steinhart was an animal in trouble. She had just suffered what had to be the most terrible day in her life. Half-strangled in fishermen's nets, towed behind a boat with a heavy fishhook through her jaw, and finally jounced around in a water-filled box on the back of a truck, she would be groggy, dazed, barely conscious. If left alone in our tank, she would almost certainly die.

But if the divers "walked" her, which in this case meant swimming her around the big reeftank, this would push water down her throat, making her breathe until she could do it on her own: artificial respiration for a shark. Huh! I wasn't going to give her mouth-to-mouth!

Adjusting my weight belt, and splashing my fintip in the water at the foot of the stairs, I tried to think if there was anything else I needed. Oh, yes, definitely—a shark stick—a two-foot length of inch-thick stainless steel (taken from a gate broken by a killer whale's bite) with a blue bicycle-handle grip glued to one end. I stuck one loosely under the loop of my belt and practiced pulling it out like a sword. I liked that part. I was not sure exactly what I would do with the stick against an excited white shark, but it was solid and comforting next to my stomach.

I was supposed to take over from the diver who was presently in the tank. I ducked down into the water and felt the surface close over my head. Out into the eerie green light I swam. My arms and legs felt very long, like bait. I pulled my arms in close and my legs together, swimming with just my hands and fins. I considered holding the shark stick in my hand but was afraid I would be laughed at, so I kept it tucked behind the quick-release buckle of my weight belt.

Where were they? All I could see was one of our artificial reefs, big as a hill, and directly before me a large school of kelp bass. Suddenly they scattered in all directions as something huge burst through them!

I pulled out the shark stick so quick my belt almost fell off.

But it was only old Chopper, our giant loggerhead, five hundred pounds of frantic-swimming sea turtle, hustling away from one of the very few predators who could give her trouble. Even an inch-thick armored shell is insufficient protection against a bite like the blow of an axe.

Then I saw them: the man and the great white shark. The human, Dave Worcester, a killer-whale trainer, was powerfully built, with a weight-lifter's arms and shoulders. But he did not loom large above the beast he held.

The white shark was beautiful. I had not been prepared for that. The dead animals I had seen photographed on the beach or fishermen's boats had been flattened by gravity, crushed by their own weight. Dead, the animals had seemed distorted, squashed, ugly. But alive and moving, the female white shark was graceful, magnificent, a work of living art.

Everything about her seemed designed to fit together in one smoothly functioning unit: from conical snout-tip to cavernous chest to crescentic half-moon tail. She was structured for power and torrents of speed, built for the charge and the kill. Her mouth was very nearly as wide as the width of her torso. One glance at the terrible notch-edged white teeth was enough to know she would be fierce and unsympathetic when aroused. The ultimate predator among fish, the great white fights the giant mammals of the sea, like Steller's sea lions, bigger than swimming grizzly bears. No small-mouthed shark could thin those herds, I thought as I swung wide around her forest of teeth.

Approaching from the back, I tapped the diver on the shoulder. His head yanked around and his eyes bulged white behind the mask. Then he realized it was just his replacement and raised his hand in the thumb-and-circled-forefinger okay sign. He flippered away to go get some rest, leaving me alone with the shark. I would not have objected if he had wanted to stay.

Feeling very unprepared for this, I put my hands on the shark's broad, rough back. The muscles underneath felt like the columns that hold up buildings. Her skin was smooth as I slid one bare hand back to grip her dorsal fin, but when I pushed the other hand forward to guide her head, the skin teeth, or denticles, dug into my fingertips. No wonder shark-skin was once used for the handles of swords. That grip was not going to slip.

I pushed her head with one hand and pulled her black-fringed dorsal with the other, and the white shark swam. Slowly. It was hard work for me, like pushing a lawn mower uphill through weeds. The shark was heavy and wanted to sink. She moved with an appearance of effort, as if she was almost asleep, groggy with oxygen deprivation. She must not be getting enough water down her throat and over her gills to let her breathe properly. I swam faster, hauling her heavily along, laboring to increase the flow of water through her open mouth. It seemed to help. She swam—slowly—but she was definitely moving on her own, making small independent mo-tions, steering us in different directions.

For a long time nothing much happened. The situation be-gan to seem unreal, as though I were pushing a surfboard or a sandpaper-covered model of a shark. I leaned forward to look at her face.

Her lower jaw flexed in a half-chewing motion as though testing the equipment—those serrate-edged teeth which could slip so easily into flesh. Her wide-slatted leathery gill covers, five on a side, flared out and contracted, partially under her muscular control. As I leaned forward I could also see one of

her eyes. White shark's eyes are said to be expressionlessly
black. Hers were. But there was also a faint mist of blue, a chill
and covering color, over the black eyeball. It was the eye Death
would have, if Death were a fish. The eye looked back and saw
me. I returned to my position and did not look front again.

from SEVENGILL

Help for Henry

MARGARET GOFF CLARK

On April 17, 1976, a young male manatee was picked up with a crab trap line around his left flipper and taken to Sea World of Florida for emergency treatment.

Henry, as he was named by rescuers, came from the Indian River near Titusville on the east coast of Florida. When he reached Sea World his flipper was so swollen and infected the veterinarian who was called in to examine him feared it would have to be amputated. At once the doctor treated the wound that encircled the flipper with antiseptics and administered antibiotics.

That first day Henry was in the pool at Sea World, although he was offered food, he did not eat. The place was new to him and no doubt he was in pain from his badly injured flipper.

The manatees' favorite food, underwater grasses, was not available at Sea World, so the staff improvised. The next day a tempting salad bar was spread out in the pool. Knowing that manatees usually prefer to eat plants from the bottoms of the rivers, Sea World staff members not only floated iceberg lettuce, endive, escarole, and romaine lettuce on top of the water, they also threaded the same type of food on a nylon rope on the floor of the pool where it was weighted and tied down.

Henry made it clear that he was hungry. In spite of his injured flipper, he dived to the bottom and began to eat. That day he devoured approximately five and one-half pounds of food. For his first week at Sea World he ate from the bottom of the pool. After that, he began feeding from the surface.

According to the report prepared by Edward D. Asper and Stan W. Searles of the Sea World staff, these were the foods offered to Henry in the order of his preference: (1) romaine lettuce (2) iceberg lettuce (3) endive (4) escarole, cabbage, spinach (5) carrot tops (6) water hyacinths. Henry ate water hyacinths only when they were the sole food in the pool, and then he just sampled the roots.

When Henry's wound was healed, he had good use of his flipper and was eating well, so the Sea World animal specialists decided to release him. During his stay of less than three months at Sea World, the manatee had gained fifty pounds.

In July he was painlessly freeze-marked on his back with a capital H to make it possible to keep track of him when he returned to the wild.

On July 9, 1976, Henry was released in the Indian River near the capture site. On many occasions after this, officers of the Florida Marine Patrol observed him swimming there.

from THE VANISHING MANATEE

Saving Corky

GEORGEANNE IRVINE

It was a stormy spring day. A baby seal was alone on a San Diego beach. His mother was nowhere in sight. The baby seal was hungry. There was no one to feed him. There was no one to protect him from harm. Surely he would die if help did not come soon.

Some people came by and saw the frightened little animal. He seemed glad to have company, even if it wasn't seal company.

The people called the California Department of Fish and Game. Officers came out to help. The officers searched and searched, but they could not find the mother seal.

The officers picked up the baby and packed him in a crate. He rode in the truck for half an hour, and then he reached his new home at the San Diego Zoo. From then on, the baby seal was known as Corky.

As soon as he arrived, Corky saw his first veterinarian and had his first check-up. Corky was put on the scale. He weighed twenty-four pounds.

For one month, Corky had to stay away from the other animals to make sure he did not have any diseases that would make the others sick. He lived in the zoo hospital in his own cage with its own little pool. He had all the fish and squid he wanted. And the hospital workers were very friendly.

After a month, Corky left the hospital and met some new friends. He moved in with a sea lion named Mickey. Corky and Mickey shared a pen with a long swimming pool. Sea lions and seals are closely related. But they are not the same animal.

Corky also met Bennie Kirkbride, a sea lion trainer. Bennie teaches sea lions how to shake hands, chase balls, and do other things. These are called behaviors.

Seals become very attached to the people who feed them. Bennie gave Corky lots of fish, so Corky followed Bennie everywhere.

Each morning, Bennie cut fish for the sea lions. Each morning, Corky would wait at Bennie's feet. Corky hoped that a piece of fish would fall his way.

One day, Corky started pawing at Bennie's leg for fish. To Bennie, this meant that Corky was ready for some lessons.

First, Bennie taught Corky how to shake hands with his flipper. Bennie touched Corky's flipper with his hand, whistled, and gave Corky a piece of fish. In only a few minutes, Corky learned that the whistle meant he had done something right, and a piece of fish was coming his way. . . .

Corky grew bigger and bigger as he gobbled more fish. Within a year, he was a roly-poly sixty pounds. That's when Corky met some new trainers: Kathy Marmack, Carlee Robinson, Heidi Ensley, and Amy Wing. They wanted Corky for their new zoo show called "Animal Chit-Chat."

During the show, the trainers walked the animals on stage one at a time and talked about them to the audience. Some of the animal performers were Daphne the emu; Arusha the cheetah and his pal, Anna, a golden retriever; Rufus, a girl wolf with a boy's name; and Irving, an eight-foot-long indigo snake with a friendly personality.

Corky performed the same routine for each show. He shook hands, rolled over, applauded, and said his prayers. Kathy also taught him some new behaviors: how to fetch a tennis ball out of the pool and how to wave hello and good-bye. And all on his own, Corky made funny noises. He quacked like a duck, and gurgled and gargled like a garbage disposal. . . .

Then one day, Corky missed some of his cues during an "Animal Chit-Chat" show. Kathy tossed a tennis ball into the seal pool, pointed, and said, "Corky, get that ball out of the pool!" Corky was usually in and out of the water like a flash, with the ball clenched tightly between his teeth. But this time, Corky seemed confused. He dragged himself around on stage before he jumped into the water. He didn't pick up the ball. He couldn't even find it.

Kathy asked Corky to shake hands. He lifted his flipper, but couldn't find Kathy's hand to shake it. Something bad was happening.

Corky always waited patiently for his trainers to drop little pieces of fish into his mouth. But then he started to grab for the fish. He almost nipped his trainers' fingers.

Corky became very snappy toward the sea lions. When he and Mickey were fed together, Corky tried to hog all of the fish for himself.

Kathy and the others worried that Corky had been working too hard in the shows. Maybe he needed a vacation. They gave Corky a few weeks' rest.

Dr. Jane Meier, a zoo veterinarian, visited Corky while he rested. Dr. Meier examined him. She put medicine in his eyes and looked closely. Corky had become blind.

Corky had developed cataracts in his eyes. A cataract is the clouding of the lens. Everything looked shadowy to him.

An operation would be too dangerous. Corky could die. The trainers were all very sad.

But Bennie knew what to do. He knew that even in the ocean, blind seals and sea lions can survive. Just as blind people learn to live without sight by depending on their other senses, so do seals and sea lions. Corky would be all right, but his trainers had to change the way they worked with him.

Before he was blind, Corky heard and saw his cues. Now he had to learn to hear and feel his cues.

In a strong, powerful voice, Kathy asked Corky to give her his flipper to shake hands. She reached down and touched his flipper so he could easily find her hand and shake it.

Corky didn't get little pieces of fish as a reward anymore. He was fed the whole fish. The trainers dangled the fish so it touched Corky's whiskers. Seal whiskers are very sensitive. Corky could feel that a fish was coming. He did not have to grab anymore.

Corky's whiskers also helped him find his tennis ball in the water again. Corky had to already be in the water. Kathy called out his old cue loudly and clearly. "Corky, get that ball out of the pool." Then she threw the ball into the pool as hard as she could so it made a BIG splash. Corky listened carefully for the splash and used his whiskers to feel the little waves the ball created when it hit. Most of the time, Corky found his tennis ball.

Corky learned a new way to find his trainers, too. Before Corky was blind, he looked for the trainer who was calling him, flopped out of the pool, and slid right over to her for his fish reward. Now, when a trainer wanted him, she yelled extra loudly, "Corky, out of the pool! Corky, come here!" She continued to call as she tapped her foot on the stage. The foot-tapping was a new cue for Corky. It helped him find his way to his trainer. Soon, Corky was out of the pool and sliding across the stage for his fish.

In only four months, Corky could perform all of his old behaviors. Once again, he could shake hands, roll over, say his prayers, and jump over the hurdle in the seal pool. Corky learned how to use feeling and hearing in place of eyesight. As a special reward, Corky received a new toy—a rubber duck that squeaks. Now Corky is happy again. He has a big pool to swim in, plenty of fish to eat, and a whole zoo full of friends to love.

from THE TRUE STORY OF CORKY, THE BLIND SEAL

BACKYARD NEIGHBORS

"Maybe,
a little,
like meeting God
through feather, fur, or fluttery thing."

SHARON KUNING

$\mathcal{Y}$ou don't have to live in the country to be close to wildlife. It's everywhere, from squirrels that run up and down the fire escapes of tall apartment buildings to raccoons that raid suburban trash cans. Perhaps you feed pigeons on your lunch hour, or keep a safe distance from the skunk that comes to your bird feeder at night. And don't forget the barn cats and wild cats that appreciate your handouts but won't let you own them.

As we learn how these animals use their God-given abilities, we become much more aware of our own.

The Alley Behind Our House

NATHAN ZIMELMAN

An alley ran along the back of our house. Flowers that weren't found anywhere else in town grew here. The grass was high and always swayed, even with only the tiniest of breezes.

Pink noses twitched. Gray forms hurried. Grasshoppers hopped. Bees bumbled. Butterflies inspected the flowers. Kids prowled about seeking adventures. The alley was a place where adventures could be found.

Herman, our family cat—who we tried to keep inside—kept sneaking out into the alley.

It was a fine place . . .

"It is a horrible place!" That's what Ms. Millicent Chillington said. We kids called her "Ms. Nosey," but no so she could hear us. She went from house to house, thrusting out a paper. "Sign on the line and we will make the City Council cover this alley with asphalt, the way a proper alley should be," she said.

Most people were afraid to disagree with Millicent Chillington, so lots of neighbors signed her paper. She didn't ask us kids to sign. We didn't count, I guess.

"We kids like the alley the way it is," I complained to my father.

"Not to worry," he said. "The City Council won't do anything. They never do."

But he was wrong. The first day of summer vacation, big men turned up with big machines. They scraped the alley down to hard-packed dirt where it seemed like nothing could possibly grow. Then trucks drove in, loaded with gravel and asphalt. When the last machine left, the alley was shiny and black—and empty.

Nobody walked down the alley. Nobody drove down it. Unless somebody wanted to go no place in a hurry, there was no reason to. There was nothing to see there.

Fall came, and I started middle school. Many winters and springs and summers and falls went by. My friends and I went to high school and college and then moved away from the neighborhood.

The winters did things to the asphalt, such as cracking it up. Then springs came, full of showers and sunshine. Seeds floated in, wedging into the cracks. Buds peered out. After a few more years, it became hard to see the asphalt of the alley through all the blossoms.

Grass waved in the breeze. Pink noses twitched. Gray forms hurried. Grasshoppers hopped. Bees bumbled. Butterflies inspected the flowers.

Visiting my parents one beautiful summer day, I opened the back door. Their new kitten scooted out before I could stop him. "Meow," he called, which said it all, as he entered the magic of the alley that ran along the back of our house.

from RANGER RICK

Who Owns This Place, Anyway?

WALTER HARTER

When we bought our old house in the country, we discovered that someone else was already in possession: a raccoon. We named him Napoleon, shortened to "Nappy," for he was a tyrant. The property had been empty for more than a year, and Nappy considered it his and us the trespassers. We tried to chase him away, and he retaliated by overturning our garbage cans, ripping tiles from the roof, and even biting through the telephone wires.

Being city folk, we'd had very little to do with wild animals. But we fought back as well as we could, even having him trapped several times and taken away to wilder country. But he always returned, and with renewed vigor continued his attempts to rid his "home" of us usurpers. It became a battle, with frayed nerves on at least one side—ours. We shrank from a suggestion that he be destroyed. But what could we do?

Finally, an elderly farmer, who had been an interested observer of our war with Nappy, explained the facts of country living to us. "Try tolerance," he suggested. "And give him a few marshmallows from time to time. There's plenty of room for him and you to live here in peace—if you respect each other's privacy."

And it has worked. We have learned that all God's creatures have a right to space in His world. There's room for all, with patience and tolerance. And Nappy seems to understand that, too, for he has become a model tenant.

Or are we the tenants and he the landlord?

The Fox

CHRIS FERRIS

8:30 a.m. At Holmoak Lane, en route for home. Met a man I know well by sight who told me a fox was snared up on the bank there. At night, going to Ashcroft Woods, I sometimes see badgers cross the tarmac at this point to follow the up-and-over path on the bank and so under the wire. Sure enough, a fox was caught by its hindquarters in a *badger* snare. It was meant to pass over the larger animal's snout and tighten where the slender neck meets the body, but in the smaller creature it had passed straight on to the pelvis. Fortunately, it was not made from cutting wire, but insulating cord. The man returned with a pair of pincers, so whilst he set to on the wire, I kept the little vixen occupied—stroked her head and made the soft contact call. The man was, at first, anxious that the animal shouldn't bite him but I, to my own surprise, found calming this stranger fox quite easy. Gently, with one hand still stroking, I ran the other under her belly and took the strain of the cord, gradually easing her body backwards. Although she would be bruised from her earlier efforts to escape, she wasn't cut. This wire cord was meant to hold and secure, not damage the animal. How beautiful these creatures are—always very interested in foxes unknown to me. My companion remarked that he had seen this type of snare before, fixed at this part of the fence.

At last she was free and I felt the tension on my hand relax—the man and I grinned at one another. As I gently took my hands away, the one from under her belly felt wet, and glancing down I saw milk on my palm! This was a lactating vixen with cubs to feed. Her sharp little face looked at us briefly, then off she raced—nothing much wrong with her! Halfway across the field, she turned and stared back at us, gave herself a quick shake, then casually trotted away. We scrambled back down the bank together laughing. It's a marvellous feeling, releasing an animal unharmed—and the way that vixen moved, she would soon be back feeding her cubs.

from THE DARKNESS IS LIGHT ENOUGH

The Invader

CAROL HATHORNE

"*It bit* me!" The young woman, coming through the vestry door with her fiancé, let out an enormous scream.

"W-what?" Standing there in my cassock, ready to welcome the St. Benedict's marriage preparation class, I stared from her to the flagged stone floor. Just in time to see a small, furry rodent shoot between us.

"A rat!" I immediately thought, and shuddered. But the young man, holding his fiancée's finger aloft—a finger showing tiny pin-pricks of blood—said: "It's a ferret! I thought something was following us across the graveyard!"

"Close the door, Reverend," he instructed me urgently, "before it gets into the church!"

Already seated in the grand, pillared nave of St. Benedict's parish church, Netherley Bank's "cathedral of the Black Country", were a dozen couples, waiting, with varying degrees of interest and impatience, for the preparation session to begin. They were all due to be married that summer and autumn, and for many of them, this was their first time in church.

Their heads shot up as if by a signal as I catapulted backwards through the inner door and slammed it firmly shut.

"You'll have to excuse me," I told my waiting congregation, "but we've got a ferret in the vestry!"

There was a moment's stunned, disbelieving silence, as if they all wondered if this might be a new evangelism ploy. Then, as I realised the incongruity of the situation, I laughed, and so did they.

"It's perfectly true," I began to explain, as I went towards the lectern. "It followed a young couple across the graveyard, and now it's bitten . . . "

"Honestly! What a performance!" The heads all turned as from behind the edifice of St. Benedict's great church organ, there emerged the bearded face and bald head of Clarke Pettisgrew, our ex-cathedral choir master and director of music.

A plump, bristling little man who made no secret of the fact that he thought the Church of England had gone insane the day it decided to ordain women, he never passed up an opportunity to try and redress the balance.

Putting down the music he had been sorting, he marched past me, saying down his nose, "I'll go and get rid of it, if you really can't bring yourself to!"

Unable to contain my curiosity, I followed him at a safe distance back into the vestry. I was just in time to see him stoop, then jump balletically about three feet into the air, his right forefinger extended painfully in front of him: "Oooer! You little . . . !"

The ferret, undeterred, darted under the nearest bench.

"What do we do now?" asked the young man who had brought the creature in while Clarke jumped around clutching his injury and talking about tetanus jabs. "I don't know the first thing about ferrets!"

"Neither do I," I confessed, "but I think I know a man who does. Just wait here while I nip to the vicarage and use the phone."

My colleague, Rev. Geoff Hanson, who lived at St. Benedict's vicarage next door was out at a school governor's meeting, but his wife, Jane, let me in. After listening open mouthed to my rather garbled account of the night's events, she agreed we should definitely send for the verger.

Tom Jenkins had been verger at St. Benedict's for over forty years. A somewhat wizened octogenarian, he knew everything and everybody in Netherley Bank, and was a self-confessed jack of all trades.

He turned up on his rusty bike just as I finished the marriage preparation class and was seeing all the couples but one off the premises, the ferret couple having gone with Clarke to the local Russets Road hospital.

"E's bin attracted by the light, see, vicar," he said knowingly as, puffing a little, he got on his hands and knees in front of the bench. "Probl'y bin left down sum rabbit 'ole over the bonk."

I stared in surprise at the tortoise-like face close to mine. "You mean people still use them for catching rabbits?" I asked.

In spite of the returned greenery that came as a result of losing its industry to waves of recession, Netherley Bank couldn't, by any stretch of the imagination, be called rural.

"Oh, ar," Tom assured me with a grunt. "Plenty o' good rabbitin' an rattin' round 'ere, vicar! Allus 'as bin!"

Bending further, he thrust his gloved hand under the bench. "Come on, beaut. I wo' 'urt yer!"

"E'll come wi' me now," he whispered, putting his face close to mine again a few moments later. "Just goo out an' switch the light off, will yer, vicar, an' leave room fer me to run out wi' me torch?"

I nodded gravely, scrambled to my feet in the hampering cassock and tiptoed to the door.

In no time at all, Tom was to be seen, running briskly across the moonlit graveyard, the torchlight spilling out a path in front of him and the ferret running, dog like, after.

"We'll, I've heard of fishers of men!" Geoff remarked, getting out of his car outside the vicarage just in time to witness the amazing scene. "I hope this isn't going to be a new trend!"

from A FERRET IN THE VESTRY

Little Warhorse, the History of a Jack-rabbit

ERNEST THOMPSON SETON

The Little Warhorse knew practically all the Dogs in town. First, there was a very large brown Dog that had pursued him many times, a Dog that he always got rid of by slipping through a hole in a board fence. Second, there was a small active Dog that could follow through that hole, and him he baffled by leaping a twenty-foot irrigation ditch that had steep sides and a swift current. The Dog could not make this leap. It was "sure medicine" for that foe, and the boys still call the place "Old Jacky's Jump." But there was a Greyhound that could leap better than the Jack, and when he could not follow through a fence, he jumped over it. He tried the Warhorse's mettle more than once, and Jacky only saved himself by his quick dodging, till they got to an Osage hedge, and here the Greyhound had to give it up. Besides these, there was in town a rabble of big and little Dogs that were troublesome, but easily left behind in the open.

In the country there was a Dog at each farm-house, but only one that the Warhorse really feared; that was a long-legged, fierce, black Dog, a brute so swift and pertinacious that he had several times forced the Warhorse almost to the last extremity.

For the town Cats he cared little; only once or twice had he been threatened by them. A huge Tom-cat flushed with many victories came crawling up to where he fed one moonlight night. Jack Warhorse saw the black creature with the glowing eyes, and a moment before the final rush, he faced it, raised up on his haunches—his hind legs—at full length on his toes, with his broad ears towering up yet six inches higher; then letting out a loud *churrr-churrr*, his best attempt at a roar, he sprang five feet forward and landed on the Cat's head, driving in his sharp hind nails, and the old Tom fled in terror from the weird two-legged giant. This trick he had tried several times with success, but twice it turned out a sad failure: once, when the Cat proved to be a mother whose Kittens were near; then Jack Warhorse had to flee for his life; and the other time was when he made the mistake of landing hard on a Skunk.

But the Greyhound was the dangerous enemy, and in him the Warhorse might have found his fate, but for a curious adventure with a happy ending for Jack.

He fed by night; there were fewer enemies about then, and it was easier to hide; but one day at dawn in winter he had lingered long at an alfalfa stack and was crossing the open snow toward his favorite form, when, as ill-luck would have it, he met the Greyhound prowling outside the town. With open snow and growing daylight there was no chance to hide, nothing but a run in the open with soft snow that hindered the Jack more than it did the Hound.

Off they went—superb runners in fine fettle. How they skimmed across the snow, raising it in little *puff-puff-puffs*, each time their nimble feet went down. This way and that, swerving and dodging, went the chase. Everything favored the Dog—his empty stomach, the cold weather, the soft snow—

while the Rabbit was handicapped by his heavy meal of alfalfa. But his feet went *puff-puff* so fast that a dozen of the little snow-jets were in view at once. The chase continued in the open; no friendly hedge was near, and every attempt to reach a fence was cleverly stopped by the Hound. Jack's ears were losing their bold up-cock, a sure sign of failing heart or wind, when all at once these flags went stiffly up, as under sudden renewal of strength. The Warhorse put forth all his power, not to reach the hedge to the north, but over the open prairie eastward. The Greyhound followed, and within fifty yards the Jack dodged to foil his fierce pursuer; but on the next tack he was on his eastern course again, and so tacking and dodging, he kept the line direct for the next farm-house, where was a very high board fence with a hen-hole, and where also there dwelt his other hated enemy, the big black Dog. An outer hedge delayed the Greyhound for a moment and gave Jack time to dash through the hen-hole into the yard, where he hid to one side. The Greyhound rushed around to the low gate, leaped over that among the Hens, and as they fled cackling and fluttering, some Lambs bleated loudly. Their natural guardian, the big black Dog, ran to the rescue, and Warhorse slipped out again by the hole at which he had entered. Horrible sounds of Dog hate and fury were heard behind him in the hen-yard, and soon the shouts of men were added. How it ended he did not know or seek to learn, but it was remarkable that he never afterward was troubled by the swift Greyhound that formerly lived in Newchusen.

from ANIMAL HEROES

Grubs and Petunia

JIM ARNOSKY

I once adopted a de-scented pet skunk named Grubs. Grubs taught me the important lesson that the best place to watch wild animals is in their natural habitat. He was a terrible house guest. Like all skunks, Grubs was nocturnal. He spent his days under a bedroom dresser. At night he came out to dig through the trash for food scraps and hunt under the sink for crickets. Grubs tore a hole in the couch fabric and made a den inside amid the stuffings and springs. He'd unpot plants and spread the soil across the rug to search for insect larvae. Personally, Grubs was fastidious. He kept his fur groomed and glistening. He always used his litter pan and, to keep it clean, he kicked its contents out onto the floor. Grubs was instinctively wild. He would not let anyone touch him. When I tried to approach, he would go through all his skunk warnings. Then he'd swing around to shoot at me, even though his barrel was empty. I finally had to take Grubs to a zoo where, happily, he was introduced to a lonely female skunk named, of all things, Petunia. That was ten years ago. Since skunks can live to be twelve years old, I figure Grubs and Petunia are now enjoying their sunset years together.

from SECRETS OF A WILDLIFE WATCHER

Sasha's Story

AMANDA J. LUKE

I'll never forget the white cat that decided to make my back porch her home several years ago. One spring morning I happened to look out my back door and saw these two white balls of fluff bouncing around in the fresh, green grass. Off to the side, but not too far away, sat a white cat, their mother.

I went out the door and tried to approach the kittens, but they ran away. I sat down on the grass to let them get used to me. The mother cat came right up—her babies watched from a distance. She let me pet her and purred contentedly when I did. She was a sweet, pretty cat that had obviously spent time around people.

Over the next couple of months I spent time getting to know this trio of white cats. I snuck food out to them (my landlord was the sort who didn't like stray cats around) and I tried to play with the kittens.

The kittens were definitely feral. The only time I ever came close to touching them, they scratched my hand badly. They were too afraid.

The mother cat, on the other hand, came over whenever I was around. She wanted me to pet and hold her. Many afternoons I would find the three of them lounging on my porch, soaking up the sunshine. They made a pretty picture.

I knew at some point I was going to have to do something about these cats. I couldn't live with the thought of them trying to survive outside when the thermometer started to drop, and I knew I couldn't take them in with my two. I called the humane society's shelter, but they said the cats had a better chance of surviving by my trying to find them a home then by bringing them to the shelter. I let things slide through the summer.

Sadly, the kittens did not survive. A neighbor found one under his porch and the other simply disappeared. It was too late for me to help them, but I could certainly do something for the mother.

I decided to get her spayed. The veterinarian told me that she was about a week into another pregnancy. We decided to spay her anyway, knowing we wouldn't be able to find homes for the kittens. Then I convinced a co-worker that she needed a pet. She named her Sasha.

I think about Sasha often and hope she's doing well. I wish I could have saved her kittens.

from CAT FANCY

Montana Mike

LYNN DONALDSON

It's 6:30 a.m., and dawn is breaking over the 30,000 acres of Jack and Ann Hirschy's Montana ranch, time for everybody to gather in the cookhouse for breakfast. Everybody, that is, except Mike, who stands outside looking forlorn, his nose pressed against the window, begging for pancakes.

But don't feel sorry for Mike; he already weighs more than 800 pounds. In fact, he's a real moose, and he'll eat just about anything, from potato chips to cat food to fruit loops—though he doesn't care for French toast. "He spits that right out," says Dave Hickman, the cook. "I think it might be the cinnamon and nutmeg."

Mike, who stands over six feet, was a baby when the Hirschys adopted him two years ago after his mother abandoned him. "He was newborn and looking for his mama, running up to the cattle trying to nurse," says Ann Hirschy, 77. "He was getting weak." Hirschy fed Mike warm milk every two hours and soon became his adopted mother. "Mike would follow me to the house," she says.

Though Mike never had a moose-size accident on her carpets, he is a bit large for a house pet, so Ann eventually had to keep him outside. "He still wants to come in," she says, and he licks the windows to get her attention.

While it is illegal to take wild animals captive, Joel Peterson, regional wildlife manager for the state's Fish, Wildlife and Parks Department, says the Hirschys (who had previously adopted a moose named Hannibal in 1989) are in the clear because Mike would have died if they hadn't taken him in. And, anyway, Mike isn't going to stay around forever; moose puberty hits soon, and then he'll take off in search of a mate, just like Hannibal did. "You miss them," says Hirschy, "but you want them to do their own thing and be happy." And to call home every now and again.

from PEOPLE

The Pet Nurse

FRED BAUER

It was a mystery how the newborn squirrel had gotten in our backyard. There were no tree nests in the area and it was certainly too young to have come there by itself. My wife Shirley helped me feed it milk from a formula we had used previously on two baby raccoons . . . and then we wondered, what should we do with it?

A check with the county wildlife office revealed that the nature center no longer cared for orphaned animals. "But some inmates over at the prison care for them. Perhaps they will help you," we were told. An hour later we handed over our squealing baby squirrel to a soft-spoken young man named Jim. He accepted our present in the prison lobby and then invited us to see the animals he was tending. They included some more squirrels, birds, a skunk, rabbits, several raccoons and a beautiful wing-damaged hawk.

Jim told us how he had served as "pet nurse" for nearly a year, helping dozens of animals before they were released. Soon he would be released himself, and would turn his job over to another inmate. "I don't know how I would have ever stood the confinement without these animals," he said, tenderly stroking a baby rabbit. "They've given so much to me."

Driving home, I thought about the discovery Jim had made behind bars . . . that the more we give, the more we receive. To learn that truth had cost him a year of his life. But then some of us never learn it in a lifetime.

Love That Never Quits

SUE MONK KIDD

$\mathcal{A}$s I walked to the mailbox that Monday, the sun was not shining. The clouds were the color of nickel, round and silver and rumbling just a little, like the rattle of a piggy bank. I glanced at the sky as two or three drops of rain splashed on top of me. I was not surprised. It seemed like it had been raining on me since I got out of bed.

The storm started when my thirteen-year-old son, Bob, and I had an argument earlier that morning. It was over something small and ridiculous. He wanted to wear an old, faded sweatshirt with cutoff sleeves to school, if you can imagine that. I insisted on the nice, new shirt his grandmother had given him for Christmas, the kind with the button-down collar and little blue monogram on the pocket. I pointed to the letters. "It's not everybody that has his initials right on his shirt," I said reasonably.

He rolled his eyes to the kitchen ceiling like something funny was written up there. "Nobody wears initials on their shirts, Mama. *Nobody!*"

Well, soon we were shouting. I mean, *really* shouting. He said terrible things. I said terrible things. Finally he yanked on the grandmother shirt. As he picked up his books, I reached over to give him a hug. Never before had he gone without a hug. But this time Bob stiffened and drew back. Then he was gone.

I hunched in my chair, stirring my coffee over and over. Dear God, had that really been the two of us going at each other like that? I felt drained. Like someone had opened the soles of my feet and emptied everything out.

The truth was, I wasn't sure how to deal with Bob anymore. Not since he'd entered the world of adolescence. He'd scarcely arrived in it, and already we were skidding into little puddles of rebellion that left me feeling exasperated and hopeless about the rest of the journey. Bob was a fine boy, a good boy, but suddenly there were days he questioned everything I said. Days he seemed to test me deliberately. There'd been so much conflict and quarreling between us lately that I was ready to throw up my hands and quit. How in the world would I get through the teenage years still ahead?

Shaking away the morning's events, I sighed and walked on, a kind of parental battle fatigue washing over me. Just ahead, the mailbox looked as defeated as I felt. Ever since a car plowed into the side of it, the pole had been bent and the door hung ajar.

Reaching inside, my hand brushed against a stack of envelopes—then something peculiar, like broom bristles. I bent down and peered inside. The day's mail sat on top of a small collection of weeds and pine straw. Odd . . . how did this get in the mailbox? Somebody's idea of a prank, I decided. I brushed out the debris, remembering the day long ago when Bob had loaded the mailbox with a water balloon, which popped, drenching the mail. I pushed the lid as closed as it would go, wishing for half a second I could have that little fellow back. The boy who liked to play pranks with water balloons—and who wore the clothes I laid out for him every single morning.

A drop of rain splatted on my nose. I shuffled toward

the house, not bothering to hurry. Suddenly parenthood felt very heavy.

That afternoon Bob breezed in from school and disappeared into his room. "How was your day?" I said, tagging behind him, trying to ignore the growing rift between us.

"Okay," he said, pulling off his shirt. He tossed the monogrammed thing on the floor at my feet. I glared at it, like he'd thrown down a gauntlet. He rummaged through his drawer for the inevitable sweatshirt with cutoff sleeves. I wheeled around to leave, then turned back. "Did you put pine straw in the mailbox?" I demanded.

He gave me a confused look, as if all his suspicions about me were now confirmed. "Never mind," I said.

But the next day when I opened the mailbox, there it was again! A smattering of pine straw, some twigs and two dead dandelions lying in the box. Once again I raked them out, blowing the dust off the mail. There was something very strange going on here.

The mystery continued all week. Each day I found a bouquet of weeds in the mailbox. And every day I whisked it out. Was it the neighborhood children up to some mischief? Or Bob? Perhaps, but I didn't bring up the subject again. As a matter of fact, I quit discussing *anything* with Bob. Every time a conflict arose I simply flexed my authority, then left the room or changed the subject. It was just easier that way.

On Saturday Bob wandered into the den where I was reading the newspaper. "Mama, can I go to the movies?" he asked. I flipped the newspaper to the theater section. The movie he was asking about was rated PG-13. The number thirteen indicated an extra note of caution to parents. I looked at my *thirteen-year-old* son. The irony was not lost on me.

"No, not this movie," I answered.

"Can't we even talk about it?" he pleaded.

"There's nothing to talk about," I said, walling myself behind the paper. It would only end up in shouting again.

"Mother, you don't understand," he cried, tearing from the room. "You don't even try!"

I sat there in the hot echo of his words, desperation rippling through me. "O God, is this how it's going to be for the next few years?" I prayed. "Please, Lord, show me what to do."

When mail time came again, I walked out as usual, and there, as usual, was the same maddening bundle of twigs and straw. When would this stop? I reached in to pull out the latest deposit, and I caught a flash of something buried inside it. It was small and round, the color of hyacinths and May sky and summer twilight. It was a tiny blue egg. *A bird's egg.*

Chirping burst from a nearby limb. There sat a bird, a piece of pine straw dangling from its beak. I gently pushed the ragged mound back inside as the truth opened to me like the unfurling of a wing. Why hadn't it occurred to me before? Had I been too preoccupied to see that the debris I'd yanked from the box all week had been the early meshing and intertwinings of a nest? I was amazed at the mother bird's tenacity. She had found our broken mailbox, and every day she had started a nest inside it. And when she returned to find it torn apart, she had tried again. Over and over again.

Suddenly I felt like God was whispering inside me. About mothering and nest-building and love that keeps on. I thought about the delicate meshing and intertwining of relationships in my home—that fragile nest of intimacy where we lived our days. How easily it unraveled! How quickly it became frayed and torn apart by the ordinary wear and tear of living. I could hear Bob's voice pleading with me: "You don't even *try.*" Was he right? Had I been so afraid of the trials of adolescence that I had retreated from the demands and quit trying? Had I somehow given up on our relationship the moment things got difficult?

I lifted my eyes to the branches above, then beyond to the curve of the sky. *With every new season of family life, new strains come,* I thought. *That's normal. Why not meet them head-on with new commitment instead of despair? The important thing is relationships—and rebuilding them as often as it takes.*

Inside, Bob sat beside his desk thumbing his globe around. "Hi," I said. He looked up at me and stared. For an instant I could see the vulnerable little boy I'd once known. But a boy growing up too, needing new independence as well as limits. "Wanna talk?" I asked. "I promise to listen."

So I sat there and listened and listened. And it was nearly the hardest work I'd ever done, but it seemed to soak up the pain and resentments between us and give us a new beginning.

Afterward we printed a small sign. "Dear Mailman," we wrote. "A mother bird has built her nest inside the mailbox. Would you deliver our mail to the door temporarily until her eggs hatch and the birds fly away?"

As we taped it to the mailbox, Bob reworded the mailman's motto: "Nothing can stop the mail from getting through. Not rain nor sleet nor snow . . . nor birds' nests," he said.

I grinned at him. Then I threw my arms around him. This time he didn't pull back. He stood right there beside the street and the battered mailbox and hugged me back. I mean *really* hugged me. And we twined our arms together like a nest that is freshly woven, and walked inside.

Before you knew it, we had three baby birds in our mailbox. Every day the mother perched atop it and filled the air with song. I always stopped to listen. For it was the song that would get me through all the teenage years and beyond—the sweet, stubborn sound of love that never quiets. At all.

SHARING OUR EARTH

"The purpose of this world is not
'to have and to hold' but
'to give and to serve.'"

SIR WILFRED T. GRENFELL

As we become better acquainted with the animals in our world, we begin to understand how important we are to each other. They remind us that we all are created by a loving God who cares deeply for each one of us. They also make us aware that each one of us is unique. We have different needs, and sometimes we have to put the needs of another before our own if we all are to survive.

One of God's Creatures

KING MSWATI III

Some of my earliest memories of childhood are of days spent with my father, the legendary King Sobhuza II, in our country's lowveld, enjoying the sights and sounds of Swaziland's wildlife and learning of the relationship between our people and the land that God gave us. On one such occasion, we were sitting within the grounds of a royal residence when a commotion of noise and activity from His Majesty's bodyguards drew our attention away from our discussion. A snake had suddenly appeared quite close to the royal group, and the king's men rushed to attack it with knives drawn and knobkerries held high. But King Sobhuza called them back. "Why are you so intent on destroying one of God's creatures?" he asked. "This place is the snake's home. He was here long before us. We are intruders on his territory. We must learn to live together in harmony with all who share our world." The snake was allowed to slither to freedom, and a young prince never forgot the wise words of his father.

from ALL THE KING'S ANIMALS

The Field Hand

STEPHANIE LALAND

In 1955, an Australian farmer called Lindsay Schmidt was driving down a country road when he encountered a roadside truck in trouble. Its driver was struggling to control a small fire that had ignited the engine. Lindsay stopped, ran to the rescue with his own fire extinguisher, and speedily put out the fire.

The grateful truck driver offered Lindsay a unit of his cargo as a reward. To his surprise, when Lindsay looked in the back of the truck, he saw twenty pairs of frightened eyes staring back at him: a group of baboons. The truck driver owned a traveling circus and used the baboons in his act. Lindsay regarded the apes curiously. Lindsay had migrated to the Australian outback only to find peace and quiet; he had no idea why he might want a baboon.

Yet at that moment, one of the baboons shyly came forward as if to greet Lindsay. It was a fateful moment. The man shared a long look with the baboon and a remarkable partnership was formed. Lindsay accepted the baboon.

When they got back to Lindsay's home, he cooked dinner and put a bowl on the floor for the baboon, whom he decided to call Johnny. Johnny looked at the table and the plate that Lindsay had set out for himself, then skeptically eyed his own dish on the floor. With a snuffle of wounded pride, Johnny picked up his dish from the floor and placed it up on the table, where he joined Lindsay. It was the first of many indications to Lindsay that he had not obtained a pet, but a companion who clearly considered himself of equal stature.

During the next few days, Johnny curiously followed Lindsay about the house and grounds, watching him do the chores. One day, when Lindsay was trying to figure out how to pick up three heavy buckets of chicken feed, Johnny grabbed a bucket and lumbered off to feed the chickens himself. Johnny performed this task so expertly that from then on feeding the chickens was Johnny's chore.

Part of Lindsay's farm routine involved driving his tractor out to the sheep pastures where he would throw down bales of hay at regular intervals. He had to drive out to each field, stop the tractor, clamber back to the trailer piled high with hay bales, heave one out to the pasture, and then return to the tractor to start over again. It occurred to him that he could cut the work time in half if he had a worker stationed on the hay trailer who could just toss the bales out at the proper intervals while he drove. Johnny had done so well with other chores, Lindsay decided to give him a try.

Johnny rode in the trailer and quickly learned to toss off hay bales at Lindsay's signal. The baboon worked the job as if he had been born to it and the sheep feeding went much faster and easier. Things proceeded perfectly until one day when the tractor hit a buried rock. The tractor lurched, throwing Lindsay forward over the front. He slammed to the earth directly in front of the tractor.

Stunned from the fall, he looked up to see the tractor rumbling inexorably toward him—in an instant he would be crushed to death. But then he heard the motor abruptly stop and the tractor halted, inches from his body. Astonished, the farmer pulled himself slowly to his feet and peered around the big tractor engine at the driver's seat. There sat Johnny, his furry hand on the ignition key. When Lindsay had been thrown in front of the tractor, Johnny had immediately leapt from the hay trailer to the rear of the tractor, climbed into the driver's seat as he had often seen Lindsay do, and turned off the engine.

The two became best friends and Johnny even learned to drive the tractor around the fields by himself. Photographs of Johnny calmly and competently driving the tractor appeared in *Life Magazine,* along with a witness' description of Johnny's careful steering back and forth.

Johnny's status as a farmhand was eventually recognized by the Australian government. Lindsay listed Johnny as an employee on his tax returns and, after an investigation, Johnny's status as "baboon field hand" was officially accepted.

from ANIMAL ANGELS

The Cinderella Dog

DIAN FOSSEY

*L*ate one afternoon . . . the Africans came back to camp carrying a black animal. I rushed to meet them, thinking they had
found yet another gorilla-trap victim. Only when the men neared
the cabin could I see that Karisoke's newest poacher victim
had a long, feebly wagging tail, two sharply pointed, alert ears,
and unusual emerald-colored eyes. The middle-aged female
dog had been caught that same morning in a wire antelope
trap and was found struggling hopelessly in the snare when the
patrol chanced upon it. The wire had ripped the dog's leg to
the bone and was working its way into the bone when the men
released her and gently carried her back to camp. With their
assistance, I dressed the horrible wound. I noticed that her
other leg bore two narrow bands of white hair several inches
above the paw, indicating that she had previously recovered
from other trap injuries.

For three months she patiently endured daily leg soakings
and bandage changes. For a while I feared her lower leg was
going to have to be amputated. Although I had encountered
many poacher dogs over the years, this was the first one that
quickly accepted the strangeness of a white person. Her friend-
liness, trust, and complete composure at being inside a cabin
with hissing kerosene lamps, typewriter, and radio sounds con-

vinced me that she, like Cindy, might have been stolen from Europeans by poachers. She adapted easily to camp life, but I could not allow her freedom outside because of the numerous antelope—particularly Primus—who also considered camp home. Hunting was in the dog's blood and there was nothing I could do to curb her impulses to chase antelope, Kima, or the chickens. Kima soon learned that the newest camp addition was controlled by a leash and took delight in jumping up and down on my cabin's tin roof to tease the dog whenever it was out.

After the leg healed, I remained in a quandary as to what to do with the dog. While I was debating her future, an ABC television crew came to Karisoke to film gorillas in mid 1979. The crew's presence was a great treat. I had a touch of bush fever and welcomed the addition of nine faces from the outside world. Among them was Earl Holliman, an actor who had long been active in American organizations concerned with humane care of domestic animals, in particular Actors and Others for Animals. After hearing the dog's story, Earl immediately named her Poacher. One night he asked me, "How do you think Poacher would like to live in Studio City, California?" From that moment on I almost believed in miracles. Within a few weeks Poacher was on a jet bound for Hollywood, where she was picked up by a veterinarian for a complete medical checkup. She continues to live there with Earl as a television star in her own right, earning sizable sums of money for animal causes by her appearances. The Karisoke staff remain justifiably proud of their part in having shaped Poacher's Cinderella fate.

from GORILLAS IN THE MIST

Valuable Lives

PATRICIA CURTIS

Marc Payne wraps the fawn in a blanket and lifts her into the arms of Mary Catherine Cupp, a high school student who is visiting the Ellenville Center and who has gone with Marc on this errand of mercy. Mary Catherine sits in the backseat of the car with the fawn.

"Try to keep her calm so she won't get upset and thrash about," Marc advises. The little animal is very frightened. She has endured a terrifying twelve hours or more. She was harassed by dogs, separated from her mother, and chased onto some people's property. In her frenzy and confusion, she ran up against the house and backed into a large exhaust fan in the wall. She has several cuts on her body from the fan.

The couple who lives in the house rescued the fawn and called the local SPCA, which in turn telephoned Lifeline for Wildlife. It took Marc over an hour to drive to the house.

Marc thanks the couple and starts back toward Ellenville. The fawn lies quietly on Mary Catherine's lap, exhausted.

Suddenly, as Marc rounds a curve, he notices an animal lying in the middle of the highway. Slowing down, he sees that it is a woodchuck, trying feebly to move. Marc is anxious to get the fawn to the farm as soon as possible, but the woodchuck will surely get hit again and again by cars if it's left where it is.

Marc pulls off to the side of the road and gets out. Mary Catherine stays in the car with the fawn. "Be careful, Marc," she says nervously. Traffic is coming fast.

Marc considers the situation: how to rescue the animal before it is run over, without getting hit himself? The road is too narrow to allow him to stop in the middle while he picks up the woodchuck. He decides he'll have to take the risk and make a run for it.

He waits until there is a little opening in the traffic, then dashes across the road, stooping in the middle and making a grab for the animal as he passes it. He misses.

Standing on the other side, Marc feels his adrenaline rising. There is no letup in the traffic. Then he sees another gap and thinks he can make it. This time as he passes the woodchuck, he scoops it up and gets across the road without a second to spare.

"Good job," breathes Mary Catherine as he returns to the car carrying the animal. "I was watching out the back window, and when you missed the first time, I couldn't look anymore."

The woodchuck doesn't appear to be crushed anywhere on its body, but seems dazed. Marc lays it in a box on the floor of the car and continues on to Ellenville.

Several student interns come out to the car as he parks under a tree. "I think we should put the fawn in seclusion and let her calm down a little before we take her on to the hospital," Marc tells them. "She may go into shock if we do any more to her now."

The interns stand back as Marc takes the baby animal from Mary Catherine's arms and carries her into the barn. Like all fawns, she is an enchanting little creature, but the students know better than to follow and watch her.

Marc washes the fawn's wounds quickly with clean water from the faucet and then puts her in an out-of-the-way spot, covering her cage with a tarpaulin. He plans to offer her milk formula from a baby bottle, but right now it is more important to leave her in peace and quiet for a while.

Marc goes back to his car to tend to the woodchuck. But when he looks in the box, it's empty!

"Hey—did anybody move the woodchuck?" he yells. But all the interns have returned to their chores—there is nobody around. Ria Schwartz, the assistant manager of the Ellenville Center and Marc's assistant, comes down from the porch where she had been doing some paperwork.

"Could it have simply walked off?" she asks. The car door had accidently been left open after Marc removed the fawn.

"But that woodchuck was out cold!" replies Marc. "I thought it would stay that way for a while." Marc and Ria search the grass and bushes for a long time. No woodchuck is to be found.

"I guess it came to while I was busy with the fawn and decided not to wait around," Marc finally decides. "Well, if it was in good enough shape to climb out of the box and take off so completely, it must have been okay."

So the wildlife population at the farm is increased by only one animal instead of two this afternoon.

The following morning, the fawn drinks a baby bottle of milk formula before she is driven to the hospital. Dr. Lerman discovers that, fortunately, the cuts from the blower fan are fairly superficial. Eventually, the animal will be brought back to the farm to convalesce, and later in the summer, when she is well, she'll be taken to a protected (no hunting) wilderness area and released.

Lifeline for Wildlife always releases animals in areas where hunting and trapping are prohibited. Though most state parks nationwide are open to these activities, there are several within driving distance of Ellenville where animals can be given their freedom in relative safety, protected at least from bullets, arrows, and traps.

from ALL WILD CREATURES WELCOME

Where the
Wild Things Are

TUFTS UNIVERSITY SCHOOL OF VETERINARY MEDICINE
with VICKI CROKE

---

*O*n a far corner of the Tufts campus, there is a little brown house where a steady stream of 1200 to 1500 patients a year arrive in shoe boxes, blankets and towels. This is the veterinary school's Wildlife Clinic, where injured chipmunks, mice, owls, turtles, deer, hawks, swans and mink—among others—are brought in for treatment. These patients have been hit by cars, shocked by power lines or punctured by bullets and arrows.

Students studying wildlife medicine come to the clinic to learn the techniques and tricks of the trade vital to saving these creatures. They discover there are seasonal patterns in the kinds of cases they see.

There is injured-baby season (spring through summer); mishaps during hunting season (fall); botulism season (summer), when animals consume food containing deadly bacterial toxins; and starvation or dehydration season (winter).

New vets also learn critical facts about different species. For example, cormorants, which are diving birds, do not have external nostrils. That's important to know, because were a vet to tape a cormorant's beak shut to work on it, the bird would barely be able to breathe. Another important bit of information: when cornered, these birds aim their beaks for the eyes, so staffers wear safety goggles.

There is also a technique for handling wild birds. One day Dr. Elizabeth Stone is in the basement giving three female students pointers on getting a red-tailed hawk out of a cage.

One student reaches into a large wooden enclosure about chest high and makes a grab with two large leather gloves. A cloud of tiny down feathers shoots out like the residue of some pillow fight. "Be careful," Stone says. "When you go to grab him, he'll go up. So anticipate that."

After a second attempt, the gloved hands emerge with the hawk, hanging upside down. The student carefully turns the bird upright and holds its feet and wings.

"Keep his feet away from your stomach," Dr. Stone warns. "And keep his face away from your chest." They can nip.

Everyone winces and laughs.

The four women bring this majestic creature to one of the operating rooms on the first floor. The bones of his right wing had been broken, and he has already had pins placed in the injured wing. Today the hawk will be anesthetized so that he can receive physical therapy—his wing will be stretched ever so gently.

The students lay him on a thick pink towel atop a stainless-steel table. Lying on his back, the bird's cream-colored chest and belly, flecked with brown markings, are exposed. A plastic mask is fitted over his beak, and the anesthesia is pumped in. The bird's body goes limp.

The hawk gets his therapy, is examined again and then rebandaged. Once he comes to, he is brought back to his cage and fed a dead mouse that has been spiked with antibiotics.

At the clinic, creatures some would consider too common to bother saving—like pigeons, squirrels and crows—get help. That's partly because the students need to learn on something, and the thinking is: better not to learn on an endangered species.

Still, the medical condition of many of their patients can inspire debates among the staffers. How far should we go to try and save an animal? Does this one stand a chance?

One such case involved a chubby little porcupine who had been found in the woods too sick to run away.

The soft-looking, chocolate-colored creature lay motionless, belly down on an examining table. Not a good sign. On examination, it is clear his back leg has been shattered, possibly by a car, and his circulatory system is not delivering enough oxygen to the organs or taking away waste products properly.

Since he is a mammal and so very ill, rabies is always a concern. Although the wildlife vets have been inoculated against the disease, vaccines sometimes fail. Today no one takes any chances. Everyone wears latex gloves.

The team of vets place a heating pad under the injured animal and inject him with fluids. A tube of brown paste high in sugar and vitamins is syringed into his mouth. And then his snout is placed in a bell-shaped mask that delivers oxygen.

Lying on the examining table, the porcupine looks like a cuddly stuffed toy with two white buckteeth and slender yellow quills speckling his soft brown fur. But this appealing little creature is in terrible shape. His temperature, which should be around 100 degrees, is only 90.1.

Another heating pad is placed over him, and a hot-water bottle is put between his back legs. A neck catheter is inserted, and he receives a steady infusion of fluids. His breathing and pulse start to improve.

A student, having trouble finding a vein for a blood sample, says without irony, "It's hard to stick a porcupine."

The animal's temperature and blood-glucose levels rise, but it is clear the young creature is not getting better. Stone is beginning to think it's time to give up. . . .

A short time later the pink euthanasia solution is injected into his neck catheter. It is an unhappy moment for everyone.

At times so many hopeless cases come in that euthanasias seem countless. And yet, says Dr. Rosemarie Borkowski, "I still get really upset putting them to sleep."

The quiet, slim blond woman is the school's so-called exotics vet and has seen it all. Rose has been bitten and scratched by a wider variety of animals than the average veterinarian. She has also faced her own crisis of deciding how far to go to save an animal. One case she still remembers was that of an injured baby barred owl. The bird was brought in with a badly lacerated head and was riddled with maggots. She was so ill she couldn't hold her head up.

The clinic was busy, and Rose had been working nonstop all day. Meanwhile, the little wilted owl waited and waited. By the time she got to the bird in the evening, Rose was exhausted. Experienced technicians were telling her the baby owl was too far gone. She should put it to sleep.

Rose got out the euthanasia drug. "As I was about to inject her," she recalls, "she really began struggling. I remember thinking: *this animal still has a lot of life in her.*"

Just then a colleague came by and commented that if the owl made it and could not be returned to the wild, they could probably find a place for her to live at a nature center near Tufts.

Feeling she couldn't make a clear decision in her exhausted state, Rose put the little bird back in the cage, and went home to bed. The next day, refreshed, she decided to try to save her. She anesthetized the baby owl, cleaned her cuts and removed the maggots.

After a few days, the weak bird finally lifted her head. She was on the mend. The staff handed her over to a one-winged barred owl, Archie, who was the center's permanent resident. The two birds bonded almost immediately.

"We have great pictures of them munching on mice together," Rose says.

Eventually the little owl grew strong enough to be released into the wild. Rose says that orphan bird taught her one of the most important lessons in medicine: to be careful not to rush clinical judgment.

from ANIMAL ER

The Bears of Summer

JACK BECKLUND

"Have you had any problems with bears?" I asked. Stan Hedstrom shrugged. My wife, Patti, and I had just bought his house on Elbow Creek. He and his brother were loading a rental van with his belongings. "We had a compost pile, and they got into that," Hedstrom said. I mentally scratched the idea of composting, and the talk turned to other matters.

Patti and I had spent the last 15 years in Florida in the newspaper business. When I first mentioned moving north, my wife replied, "You're not serious." But after two fall vacations among the colorful maples and aspens, energized by the brisk air, she changed her mind.

Our destination was Grand Marais, Minn., on the North Shore of Lake Superior. The town has one stoplight, a couple dozen tourist cabins, a few small motels and 1100 residents, including at least 20 of my uncles, aunts, cousins, nephews and nieces.

Grand Marais was the place where my grandfather put down roots after emigrating from Sweden. I had lived in the area until I was five. Here I caught my first brook trout in a hidden stream; later, my family came back for cool summer vacations or skiing in winter. In the summer of 1988, Patti and I returned to work for the local weekly newspaper, *The Cook County News-Herald,* which we later took over.

The night we moved in, I was unable to sleep, so I opened the sliding-glass door and stepped onto our back deck. I stood listening to the murmur of Elbow Creek and the far-off yip of a coyote.

I thought again about bears. I had grown up with a healthy fear of them. I remember as a boy reading *The Complete Book of Hunting,* which warned: When hungry, bears are recklessly intrusive and very dangerous. At all times of the year they are unpredictable. . . .

Fortunately, we did not see a bear on our property until our second summer in Grand Marais. The cats, startled by something outside, woke me late one night. When I went to check, there, in the dim gray light, a very large black bear was standing brazenly on the front lawn beneath the pin cherry tree. He seemed to be studying the hummingbird feeder suspended from a limb. Rising on his hind legs, he grasped the feeder in both paws, tilted it expertly and gulped down its contents.

Looking down from our deck, I began yelling and waving my arms wildly. Ramah, our black Labrador, joined me with enthusiastic barking. The bear headed south, crashing over deadfalls and breaking brush. "Whew," I exclaimed, flushed with victory. "Bet he'll be running till tomorrow morning." Was I wrong.

Perhaps it was the sound of the trash barrel being overturned. Or maybe it was the bird feeder being ripped from its moorings. Whatever it was, at 4 a.m. I awoke again. We had learned our first lesson about bears. You can scare one off, but not for long. By the time I reached the door, the damage was done, and the bear was heading down the driveway.

The next visit was the following spring, during the May

thaw. Deer came by, gaunt from a hard winter, so we had put out a pile of corn for them.

One day Patti finished her work at the office and went home early. She was excited and out of breath when she called. "You'll never believe it. A mama bear and her two cubs were at the corn pile."

Soon the bears settled in. We'd see them eating the corn during the day, and we'd hear the cubs scampering up into the trees at night. After a few edgy days, I talked with Patti. "The bears are fun to watch," I said, "but they worry me." I had wanted to start a garden, but the fear of getting between mother and cubs was a deterrent. We were also concerned that our dog would chase the cubs and end up face to face with an angry bear. We decided to scare them off.

A neighbor told us about a sure-fire solution. This consisted of filling balloons with ammonia and water, coating them with honey and hanging them from low branches. The honey lured the bears, and when they popped the balloons, they got a bitter surprise.

Great idea, I thought. By dusk we'd filled and coated eight balloons and left them hanging festively along the driveway. I could hardly wait for morning.

When Patti got up and looked out, she counted nine intact balloons scattered along the drive. "Wait a second," she said. "We only put out eight."

The bears had not only licked the honey off every balloon without puncturing any, but they had also carried one of our neighbor's balloons to our house, a distance of half a mile.

That day I called the local wildlife manager, Bill Peterson. He laughed at my story of the balloons. "You might try a slingshot," he said. "That sometimes does the trick."

We came home that afternoon with a slingshot from the Lake Superior Trading Post. During the evening I managed to hit mama bear about three times in the rump. It gave her a little sting and she seemed to get the message. Both the mother and the cubs disappeared for a day; for two days; then three. After two weeks we declared victory.

Then, one June afternoon less than a month later, a little black bear ambled casually down our driveway. A yearling, the cub weighed no more than 25 or 30 pounds. We didn't know it at the time, but our lives were never going to be the same again.

"He's just an orphan," Patti exclaimed. I watched as the small bear moved unerringly toward the pan of sunflower seeds we'd placed on a stump for birds. "Can we let him have something to eat?" she asked me, knowing full well we had worked all spring to get these animals to move.

Still wary of bears, I did note that this young scavenger was no more than half the size of our dog and figured I could deal with it. "I suppose it's okay," I said. By then Patti was already hurrying toward the front door with more seeds.

"Be careful. His mother might be lurking in the woods," I admonished. Patti barely heeded my words in her rush to get outside. She never met an animal she did not like, and was always the one to bring home stray dogs and other creatures. Now she was moving up to bears.

Seeing her, the cub at first ran to the pin cherry tree and stood upright, holding on to the trunk in case escape became necessary. From the dining-room window, I watched as Patti sat on the grass, talking quietly to the young cub. The little bear stood still for two or three minutes; then, sensing that my wife meant no harm, it dropped to all fours and edged up to the pan of seeds.

Soon it was eating cautiously just four feet from Patti. The two stayed that way for nearly a half-hour until the mound of seeds had vanished. My wife then refilled the pan and set it down on the grass. She watched as the bear resumed eating. By now, however, the bloodthirsty Minnesota mosquitoes had discovered her and she had to come inside.

"Wow!" she said as she walked through the door. "Did you see that? We've got a female cub out there. Isn't she perfect?" I think we should call her 'little' something. How about Little Bit?"

For the next two days Patti would watch for the cub to make an appearance, cover herself with insect repellent and then go outside. Eventually the young bear let Patti sit directly across from the pan while she ate.

In general, black bears are gentle and shy. If confronted by a human, they will almost invariably retreat. Still, one must never forget they are strong, powerful creatures. We knew enough never to come at a strange bear aggressively—as indeed no one should—and we always approached Little Bit with care.

After each encounter Patti would return, thrilled at the animal's growing trust in her. On the third day we decided to lure the cub away from the driveway to our back yard. My truck's comings and goings frightened her. Then, too, we loved to watch a family of deer chase each other around on our front lawn. With the cub out of sight, they'd be more likely to stay.

Our strategy was simply. Sunflower seeds ranked right after honey as this bear's favorite food, so all we had to do was to move the pan. Wherever it went, the bear soon followed.

We have a 32-foot-long deck at the back of our house; it stands at a carefully calculated one story off the ground. A sliding-glass door leads into our living room, and a flight of stairs leads to the yard below. We placed the seed pan at the top of the steps, and Little Bit soon joined us whenever we sat outside to eat lunch. Before long my wife was able to touch and even ruffle the little black bear's coat.

One day not long after we had established this routine, Patti looked outside. "Oh, my gosh, what's happened to you?" I heard her say, as I glanced up to see the mangiest cub imaginable walking toward me.

When Patti opened the door, the animal made a hasty retreat, flying across the deck and down the stairs. It wasn't until the scrawny cub literally collided with Little Bit at the bottom of the steps that we realized that this bear was a stranger.

In time we learned the youngsters were not orphans. Mother bears routinely abandoned their cubs in June of their second summer. They did this before mating again. Our two cubs had probably only recently been set adrift.

Over the next few days the two became friends and began returning together. I shook my head, thinking about how I should have drawn the line at one. But before I could say a word, Patti had named the newcomer Skinny, and I knew that was it.

By August Little Bit and Skinny were inseparable and growing rapidly. Thanks to my wife's heaping bowls of sunflower seeds, they put on weight and became a pair of plump fur balls.

I was amazed at the quantity of seed the bears consumed. The 50-pound bags were disappearing at a rate that threatened our budget. "Don't they seem to be eating an awful lot?" I asked Patti one day.

"Maybe they're trying to get ready for hibernation," she said.

Two nights later we discovered the truth. As dusk fell, Little Bit and Skinny wandered out to our side yard and were joined by three other bears.

Now we had five.

It didn't end there. By September we had accumulated nine cubs. They seemed to understand that they were safe with us. That led to the name we've called our place ever after: the Sanctuary.

On September 1 bear-hunting season began and we started to worry. Hunters set out meat, fish, honey, dog food, syrup, jam or any other food that might lure a bear. Then they sat in tree stands overlooking their bait and shot the unsuspecting animals as they ate.

Although I had been a hunter for many years, I'd never hunted like this—to my mind it requires neither skill nor sportsmanship. Fortunately, bears are highly intelligent. After the first weekend of the season, they catch on quickly, and very few are killed later in the month.

By mid-September our pack of juveniles had managed to avoid the hunters, but they were nonetheless starting to dwindle. By October all of them, including Little Bit, had left to hibernate. As the cold weather set in, we worried about Little Bit. Would she survive the ravages of the cold?

She returned safely in the spring of 1991 for another summer of companionship and free food. And yet when the next winter came, we fretted all over again.

On Memorial Day, 1992, our prayers were answered. Little Bit coolly walked up on our deck with Skinny close behind. She looked directly at Patti as if to say, "Of course I'm here. What did you expect?" Then she sat down, legs splayed out, and commenced eating seeds as though she'd never been away.

Skinny, by contrast, had changed. He had learned to enjoy the company of other bears and began to seek them out more.

Every week or so he would go off alone for three or four days on what we called Skinny's Walkabouts.

On his increasingly short visits with us, we could see he was not only more independent, but also bigger and more aggressive. Although he still trotted after Patti like a large black puppy, he was not so relaxed around other males, including me.

One afternoon on the deck, I made a move to get up to go inside, and he spun around with his paw and cuffed my shirt, barely missing my side. I'm sure this was a natural defensive reaction, but thereafter I moved a lot more deliberately around him.

In June Little Bit also gave up her stay-at-home ways and began to roam. One day Patti was on the deck when she called to me. "Jack, you better come out and take a look at this. You're not going to believe it."

Little Bit was sitting near my wife, her legs stuck through the railing, licking some sunflower seeds. As I peered over her and down into the yard, I saw him—a very big male. The bear cocked his head up, almost squinting in the sunlight, looking for his mate.

After finishing her snack, Little Bit ambled to the stairs. The male ventured up two steps and carefully smelled her neck and muzzle. She licked his nose—together they looked the picture of newfound love. Then she pushed past him and headed down the trail leading to the creek.

We watched the couple until they disappeared from view. "Wow," said Patti. "I feel like a mother-in-law."

I laughed. "You're right. She brought her new boyfriend home to show him off."

As the summer wore on, we saw other signs that our bears were maturing. One day Skinny vanished as abruptly as he'd appeared. Either he'd found a lovely female bear to court or he'd gotten himself in some kind of trouble. Whatever the cause, he never came back.

That September we also started to notice changes in Little Bit's personality. She seemed to prefer our company to that of the other bears. While the males roughhoused on the grass, she sat with us, often eating sunflower seeds and nuts from Patti's hand. Sometimes my wife would put a few nuts on the deck or the bench seat, only to have Little Bit ignore them and nuzzle her to be hand-fed. The wild creature's touch was as gentle as a butterfly's.

Though she was growing closer to us, we suspected that because of her new boyfriend, Little Bit probably would be returning with a family the next summer. We called a bear expert and asked a question that had been troubling us: How would Little Bit behave toward us if she had a cub or cubs to protect? Would she still be the same bear?

"Yes, indeed," he assured us. "How she acts around you without cubs is how she'll act with cubs. If she trusted you before, she'll trust you after." With that advice, we started the long vigil until spring.

After a winter of expectation, our bears began to come back. Little Bit was among the first to arrive one spring day in 1993.

The forest was leafing out in its many shadings of light and delicate greens. Little Bit marched up to the sliding-glass door and placed her muddy paws against the glass to announce her presence. Right behind her was a gangly male cub. When Patti opened the door, the cub took one look at her, fled off the deck and ran up an old spruce tree.

During every subsequent visit, Little Bit made it clear she was happy to see us. On the other hand, her cub wanted nothing to do with us. Each time they'd stop by he'd end up running off into the woods.

Thus began a strange summer. We could see the young mother had allowed her cub, whom we named Miracle (as in "it will be a miracle if he survives"), to get the upper hand.

One day we watched as Little Bit, by now a 250-pound adult, sat at the base of an old spruce tree by the deck, waiting for her cub to come down. She had been sitting all morning and was losing the battle of wills with the stubborn youngster. Finally impatient, Little Bit stood up and began to climb up the trunk through the maze of branches.

As she approached Miracle, he looked down at her and defiantly climbed out of reach to the topmost limb, which was no more than a supple wand.

Little Bit hesitated, stopped, then retreated down the tree. At the bottom she threw herself against the trunk in obvious frustration.

Later, when Patti looked out the back door, the new mother was still lying there. The cub was up in the tree, stretched across several branches, fast asleep.

It was Little Bit's easygoing nature that allowed the cub to defy her. When she clunked deep in her throat, as mother bears do to call their young, he ignored her; instead of leading Miracle through the woods, Little Bit followed him; and when male bears threatened, she retreated with her cub, sometimes even climbing a tree behind him.

This was in contrast to every other bear we had seen. Some mothers exerted the control of a drill sergeant over their brood. All this made us wonder if Little Bit's poor parenting skills were somehow a result of our relationship with her.

As we soon saw, though, even this laid-back bear had her

limits. One day Little Bit was eating seeds from a small box we had placed on the deck. An old piece of frayed rope hung from one side of the container. Patti and I watched as Miracle grabbed the rope several times, pulling the box away from his mother. Each time, Little Bit gently reached over to retrieve it. "That is the most patient mother bear in the world," my wife said.

Eventually, the cub pushed his luck too far. He went for the rope again; but this time his mother was ready. Holding the box with one paw, she delivered a swat with the other that sent the cub tumbling head over heels.

"Wow," Patti said. "*Finally,* she let him have it." A half-hour later, Miracle followed dutifully when Little Bit got up to leave. At last the young female was starting to get the hang of this mother business.

Unfortunately, she remained timid with other animals. Though she was getting bigger each summer, Little Bit still hid behind me for protection when other adult bears appeared.

from SUMMERS WITH THE BEARS

A Walk With My Friends

JANE GOODALL

$\mathcal{T}$he coming brightness of the sun had all but vanquished the silvery, indefinite illumination of its own radiance reflected by the moon. The chimpanzees still slept.

Five minutes later came a rustling of leaves above. I looked up and saw branches moving against the lightening sky. That was where Goblin, top-ranking male of the community, had made his nest. Then stillness again. He must have turned over, then settled down for a last snooze. Soon after this there was movement from another nest to my right, then from one be hind me, further up the slope. Rustlings of leaves, the cracking of a little twig. The group was waking up. Peering through my binoculars into the tree where Fifi had made a nest for herself and her infant Flossi, I saw the silhouette of her foot. A moment later Fanni, her eight-year-old daughter, climbed up from her nest nearby and sat just above her mother, a small dark shape against the sky. Fifi's other two offspring, adult Freud and adolescent Frodo, had nested further up the slope.

Nine minutes after he had first moved, Goblin abruptly sat up and, almost at once, left his nest and began to leap wildly through the tree, vigorously swaying the branches. Instant pandemonium broke out. The chimpanzees closest to Goblin left their nests and rushed out of his way. Others sat up to watch, tense and ready for flight. The early morning peace was shattered by frenzied grunts and screams as Goblin's subordinates voiced their respect or fear. A few moments later, the arboreal part of his display over, Goblin leapt down and charged past me, slapping and stamping on the wet ground, rearing up and shaking the vegetation, picking up and hurling a rock, an old piece of wood, another rock. Then he sat, hair bristling, some fifteen feet away. He was breathing heavily. My own heart was beating fast. As he swung down, I had stood up and held onto a tree, praying that he would not pound on me as he sometimes does. But, to my relief, he had ignored me, and I sat down again.

With soft, panting grunts Goblin's young brother Gimble climbed down and came to greet the alpha or top-ranking male, touching his face with his lips. Then, as another adult male approached Goblin, Gimble moved hastily out of the way. This was my old friend Evered. As he approached, with loud, submissive grunts, Goblin slowly raised one arm in salutation and Evered rushed forward. The two males embraced, grinning widely in the excitement of this morning reunion so that their teeth flashed white in the semi-darkness. For a few moments they groomed each other and then, calmed, Evered moved away and sat quietly nearby.

The only other adult who climbed down then was Fifi, with Flossi clinging to her belly. She avoided Goblin, but approached Evered, grunting softly, reached out her hand and touched his arm. Then she began to groom him. Flossi climbed into Evered's lap and looked up into his face. He glanced at her, groomed her head intently for a few moments, then turned to reciprocate Fifi's attentions. Flossi moved half-way towards where Goblin sat—but his hair was still bristling, and she thought better of it and, instead, climbed a tree near Fifi. Soon she began to play with Fanni, her sister.

Once again peace returned to the morning, though not the silence of dawn. Up in the trees the other chimpanzees of the group were moving about, getting ready for the new day. Some began to feed, and I heard the occasional soft thud as skins and seeds of figs were dropped to the ground. I sat, utterly content to be back at Gombe after an unusually long time away—almost three months of lectures, meetings, and lobbying in the USA and Europe. This would be my first day with the chimps and I planned to enjoy it to the full, just getting reacquainted with my old friends, taking pictures, getting my climbing legs back.

It was Evered who led off, thirty minutes later, twice pausing and looking back to make sure that Goblin was coming too. Fifi followed, Flossi perched on her back like a small jockey, Fanni close behind. Now the other chimps climbed down and wandered after us. Freud and Frodo, adult males Atlas and Beethoven, the magnificent adolescent Wilkie, and two females, Patti and Kidevu, with their infants. There were others, but they were travelling higher up the slope, and I didn't see them then. We headed north, parallel with the beach below, then plunged down into Kasakela Valley and, with frequent pauses for feeding, made our way up the opposite slope. The eastern sky grew bright, but not until 8:30 a.m. did the sun itself finally peep over the peaks of the rift escarpment. By this time we were high above the lake. The chimpanzees stopped and groomed for a while, enjoying the warmth of the morning sunshine.

About twenty minutes later there was a sudden outbreak of chimpanzee calls ahead—a mixture of pant-hoots, as we call the loud distance calls, and screams. I could hear the distinctive voice of the large, sterile female Gigi among a medley of females and youngsters. Goblin and Evered stopped grooming and all the chimps stared towards the sounds. Then, with Goblin now in the lead, most of the group moved off in that direction.

Fifi, however, stayed behind and continued to groom Fanni while Flossi played by herself, dangling from a low branch near her mother and elder sister. I decided to stay too, delighted that Frodo had moved on with the others for he so often pesters me. He wants me to play, and, because I will not, he becomes aggressive. At twelve years of age he is much stronger than I am, and this behaviour is dangerous. Once he stamped so hard on my head that my neck was nearly broken. And on another occasion he pushed me down a steep slope. I can only hope that, as he matures and leaves childhood behind him, he will grow out of these irritating habits.

I spent the rest of the morning wandering peacefully with Fifi and her daughters, moving from one food tree to the next. The chimps fed on several different kinds of fruit and once on some young shoots. For about forty-five minutes they pulled apart the leaves of low shrubs which had been rolled into tubes held closely by sticky threads, then munched on the caterpillars that wriggled inside. Once we passed another female—Gremlin and her new infant, little Galahad. Fanni and Flossi ran over to greet them, but Fifi barely glanced in their direction.

All the time we were climbing higher and higher. Presently, on an open grassy ridge we came upon another small group of chimps: the adult male Prof, his young brother Pax, and two rather shy females with their infants. They were feeding on the leaves of a massive *mbula* tree. There were a few quiet grunts of greeting as Fifi and her youngsters joined the group, then they also began to feed. Presently the others moved on, Fanni with them. But Fifi made herself a nest and stretched out for a midday siesta. Flossi stayed too, climbing about, swinging, amusing herself near her mother. And then she joined Fifi in her nest, lay close and suckled.

From where I sat, below Fifi, I could look out over the Kasakela Valley. Opposite, to the south, was the Peak. A surge of warm memories flooded through me as I saw it, a rounded shoulder perched above the long grassy ridge that separates Kasakela from the home valley, Kakombe. In the early days of the study at Gombe, in 1960 and 1961, I had spent day after day watching the chimpanzees, through my binoculars, from the superb vantage point. I had taken a little tin trunk up to the Peak, with a kettle, some coffee and sugar, and a blanket. Sometimes, when the chimps had slept nearby, I had stayed up there with them, wrapped in my blanket against the chill of the night air. Gradually I had pieced together something of their daily life, learned about their feeding habits and travel routes, and begun to understand their unique social structure—small groups joining to form larger ones, large groups splitting into smaller ones, single chimpanzees roaming, for a while, on their own.

From the Peak I had seen, for the first time, a chimpanzee eating meat: David Greybeard. I had watched him leap up into a tree clutching the carcass of an infant bushpig, which he shared with a female while the adult pigs charged about below. And only about a hundred yards from the Peak, on a never-to-be-forgotten day in October, 1960, I had watched David Greybeard, along with his close friend Goliath, fishing for termites with stems of grass. Thinking back to that far-off time I re-lived the thrill I had felt when I saw David reach out, pick a wide blade of grass and trim it carefully so that it could more easily be poked into the narrow passage in the termite mound. Not only was he using the grass as a tool—he was, by modifying it to suit a special purpose, actually showing the crude beginnings of tool-*making*. What excited telegrams I had sent off to Louis Leakey, that far-sighted genius who had instigated the research at Gombe. Humans were not, after all, the *only* tool-making animals. Nor were chimpanzees the placid vegetarians that people had supposed. . . .

Above me, Fifi stirred, cradling little Flossi more comfortably as she suckled. Then her eyes closed again. The infant nursed for a few more minutes, then the nipple slipped from her mouth as she too slept. I continued to daydream, re-living in my mind some of the more memorable events of the past.

I remembered the day when David Greybeard had first visited my camp by the lakeshore. He had come to feed on the ripe fruits of an oil-nut palm that grew there, spied some bananas on the table outside my tent, and taken them off to eat in the bush. Once he had discovered bananas he had returned for more and gradually other chimpanzees had followed him to my camp. . . .

Fifi, lying so peacefully above me now, was one of the few survivors of those early days. She had been an infant when first I knew her in 1961. She had weathered the terrible polio epidemic that had swept through the population—chimpanzee and human alike—in 1966. Ten of the chimpanzees of the study group had died or vanished. Another five had been crippled, including her eldest brother, Faben, who had lost the use of one arm.

At the time of that epidemic the Gombe Stream Research Centre was in its infancy. The first two research assistants were helping to collect and type out notes on chimp behaviour. Some twenty-five chimpanzees were regularly visiting camp by then, and so there had been more than enough work for all of us. After watching the chimps all day we had often transcribed notes from our tape recorders until late at night. . . .

There was a slight movement from Fifi's nest and I saw that she had turned and was looking down at me. What was she thinking? How much of the past did she remember? Did she ever think of her old mother, Flo? Had she followed the desperate struggle of her brother, Figan, to rise to the top-ranking, alpha position? Had she even been aware of the grim years when the males of her community, often led by Figan, had waged a sort of primitive war against their neighbours, assaulting them, one after the other, with shocking brutality? Had she known about the gruesome cannibalistic attacks made by Passion and her adult daughter Pom on newborn infants of the community?

Again my attention was jerked back to the present, this time by the sound of a chimpanzee crying. I smiled. That would be Fanni. She had reached the adventurous age when a young female often moves away from her mother to travel with the adults. Then, suddenly, she wants mother desperately, leaves the group, and sets off to search for her. The crying grew louder and soon Fanni came into sight. Fifi paid no attention, but Flossi jumped out of the nest and scrambled down to embrace her elder sister. And Fanni, finding Fifi where she had left her, stopped her childish crying.

Clearly Fifi had been waiting for Fanni—now she climbed down and set off, and the children, followed after, playing as they went. The family moved rapidly down the steep slope to the south. As I scrambled after them, every branch seemed to catch in my hair or my shirt. Frantically I crawled and wriggled through a terrible tangle of undergrowth. Ahead of me the chimpanzees, fluid black shadows, moved effortlessly. The distance between us increased. The vines curled around the buckles of my shoes and the strap of my camera, the thorns caught in the flesh of my arms, my eyes smarted till the tears flowed as I yanked my hair from the snags that reached out from all around. After ten minutes I was drenched in sweat, my shirt was torn, my knees bruised from crawling on the stony ground—and the chimps had vanished. I kept quite still, trying to listen above the pounding of my heart, peering in all directions through the thicket around me. But I heard nothing.

For the next thirty-five minutes I wandered along the rocky bed of the Kasakela Stream, pausing to listen, to scan the branches above me. I passed below a troop of red colobus monkeys, leaping through the tree tops, uttering their strange, high-pitched, twittering calls. I encountered some baboons of D troop, including old Fred with his one blind eye and the double kink in his tail. And then, as I was wondering where to go next, I heard the scream of a young chimp further up the valley. Ten minutes later I had joined Gremlin with little Galahad, Gigi and two of Gombe's youngest and most recent orphans, Mel and Darbee, both of whom had lost their mothers when they were only just over three years old. Gigi, as she so often does these days, was "auntying" them both. They were all feeding in a tall tree above the almost dry stream and I stretched out on the rocks to watch them. During my scramble after Fifi the sun had vanished, and now, as I looked up through the canopy, I could see the sky, grey and heavy with rain. With a growing darkness came the stillness, the hush, that so often precedes hard rain. Only the rumbling of the thunder, moving ever closer, broke this stillness; the thunder and the rustling movements of the chimpanzees.

When the rain began Galahad, who had been dangling and patting at his toes near his mother, quickly climbed to the shelter of her arms. And the two orphans hurried to sit, close together, near Gigi. But Gimble started leaping about in the tree tops, swinging vigorously from one branch to the next, climbing up then jumping down to catch himself on a bough below. As the rain got heavier, as more and more drops found their way through the dense canopy, so his leaps became wilder and ever more daring, his swaying of the branches more vigorous. This behaviour would, when he was older, express itself in the magnificent rain display, or rain dance, of the adult male.

Suddenly, just after three o'clock, heralded by a blinding flash of lightning and a thunderclap that shook the mountains and growled on and on, bouncing from peak to peak, the grey-black clouds let loose such torrential rain that sky and earth seemed joined by moving water. Gimble stopped playing then, and he, like the others, sat hunched and still, close to the trunk of the tree. I pressed myself against a palm, sheltering as best I could under its overhanging fronds. As the rain poured down endlessly I got colder and colder. Soon, turned in upon myself, I lost all track of time. I was no longer recording—there was nothing to record except silent, patient and uncomplaining endurance.

It must have taken about an hour before the rain began to ease off as the heart of the storm swept away to the south. At

4:30 the chimps climbed down, and moved off through the soaked, dripping vegetation. I followed, walking awkwardly, my wet clothes hindering movement. We travelled along the stream bed then up the other side of the valley, heading south. Presently we arrived on a grassy ridge overlooking the lake. A pale, watery sun had appeared and its light caught the raindrops so that the world seemed hung with diamonds, sparkling on every leaf, every blade of grass. I crouched low to avoid destroying a jewelled spider's web that stretched, exquisite and fragile, across the trail.

The chimpanzees climbed into a low tree to feed on fresh young leaves. I moved to a place where I could stand and watch as they enjoyed their last meal of the day. The scene was breathtaking in its beauty. The leaves were brilliant, a pale, vivid green in the soft sunlight; the wet trunk and branches were like ebony; the black coats of the chimps were shot with flashes of coppery-brown. And behind this vivid tableau was the dramatic backcloth of the indigo-black sky where the lightning still flickered and flashed, and the distant thunder rumbled.

There are many windows through which we can look out into the world, searching for meaning. There are those opened up by science, their panes polished by a succession of brilliant, penetrating minds. Through these we can see ever further, ever more clearly, into areas that once lay beyond human knowledge. Gazing through such a window I have, over the years, learned much about chimpanzee behaviour and their place in the nature of things. And this, in turn, has helped us to understand a little better some aspects of human behaviour, our own place in nature.

But there are other windows; windows that have been unshuttered by the logic of philosophers; windows through which the mystics seek their visions of the truth; windows from which the leaders of the great religions have peered as they searched for purpose not only in the wondrous beauty of the world, but also in its darkness and ugliness. Most of us, when we ponder on the mystery of our existence, peer through but one of these windows onto the world. And even that one is often misted over by the breath of our finite humanity. We clear a tiny peep-hole and stare through. No wonder we are confused by the tiny fraction of a whole that we see. It is, after all, like trying to com-prehend the panorama of the desert or the sea through a rolled-up newspaper.

As I stood quietly in the pale sunshine, so much a part of the rain-washed forests and the creatures that lived there, I saw for a brief moment through another window and with other vision. It is an experience that comes, unbidden, to some of us who spend time alone in nature. The air was filled with a feath-ered symphony, the evensong of birds. I heard new frequen-cies in their music and, too, in the singing of insect voices, notes so high and sweet that I was amazed. I was intensely aware of the shape, the colour, of individual leaves, the varied patterns of the veins that made each one unique. Scents were clear, easily identifiable—fermenting, over-ripe fruit; water-logged earth; cold, wet bark; the damp odour of chimpanzee hair and, yes, my own too. And the aromatic scent of young, crushed leaves was almost overpowering. I sensed the pres-ence of a bushbuck, then saw him, quietly browsing upwind, his spiralled horns dark with rain. And I was utterly filled with that peace "which passeth all understanding".

Then came far-off pant-hoots from a group of chimpan-zees to the north. The trance-like mood was shattered. Gigi and Gremlin replied, uttering their distinctive pant-hoots. Mel,

Darbee and little Galahad joined in the chorus.

I stayed with the chimps until they nested—early, after the rain. And when they had settled down, Galahad cosy beside his mother, Mel and Darbee each in their own small nests close to the big one of auntie Gigi, I left them and walked back along the forest trail to the lakeshore. I passed the D troop baboons again. They were gathered around their sleeping trees, squabbling, playing, grooming together, in the soft light of evening. My walking feet crunched the shingle of the beach, and the sun was a huge red orb above the lake. As it lit the clouds for yet another magnificent display, the water became golden, shot with gleaming ripples of violet and red below the flaming sky.

Later, as I crouched over my little wood fire outside the house, where I had cooked, then eaten, beans and tomatoes and an egg, I was still lost in the wonder of my experience that afternoon. It was, I thought, as though I had looked onto the world through such a window as a chimpanzee might know. I dreamed, by the flickering flames. If only we could, however briefly, see the world through the eyes of a chimpanzee, what a lot we should learn.

from THROUGH A WINDOW

White Tiger in My House

ELIZABETH C. REED

It wasn't my husband's fault. Still, the timing could not have been worse. I was busy in the kitchen, preparing dinner for 14 guests, when he telephoned.

"Do you want the white cub now or later today?" Ted asked.

I should be used to that kind of question. My husband, Dr. Theodore H. Reed, directs the Smithsonian Institution's National Zoological Park in Washington, D.C. As a result, I've been foster mother to four hybrid bears, one grizzly cub, and two young leopards. Oh yes, and to a ring-tailed lemur that used to perch on my shoulder drinking orange juice.

Rewati, though, would be a different breed of cat—the only white tiger cub in the Americas. Ten years ago my husband had journeyed to India to escort her mother to this country. For the past decade, Mohini—Enchantress—has been one of the zoo's most popular attractions. With her blue eyes, and gray-brown stripes on whitish fur, Mohini is a mutant—a color variation of the orange Bengal tiger.

Zoo officials hoped to perpetuate Mohini's whiteness by mating her with Sampson, an uncle of hers bred from an orange Bengal mother and a white father. In 1964 they were successful. Mohini gave birth to three cubs, including a white one, but the white cub died of a virus at 19 months.

This time Mohini had been mated with another orange tiger carrying a white gene, Ramana, and eight days before my husband's telephone call she had given birth to a white female cub. Indian Ambassador Nawab Ali Yavar Jung suggested her name, Rewati, after a pure mountain stream in his country.

Mohini had been a model mother at first, but now zoo officials were worried. She had begun to lick her offspring excessively and pace nervously around the cage carrying it in her mouth. The rare and valuable cub was in danger; someone would have to take over the mother's role.

My husband felt he had no right to ask any of his associates to assume that grave responsibility. Rewati would come to our house where he could watch her closely—and I was drafted as foster mother.

That afternoon, before the dinner party, Ted brought the baby tiger home. It was hard to realize, staring at that appealing little 2½-pound bundle of fluff, that she would become a regal giant of 400 pounds or more. We scurried around the house, turning an upstairs bedroom into a nursery, complete with incubator, baby scale, and nursing bottles.

If I was a bit preoccupied that night, I'm sure the guests understood. There was at least $10,000 worth of infant tiger in that incubator upstairs. And, really, it was more than just a matter of money. Countless thousands of people had already learned of Rewati through the news media, and were eager to see her when she was old enough to return to the zoo. What if I blundered in my mother's role? There was so much that I didn't know—that no one knew—about hand-raising a white tiger cub!

Of some three dozen white tigers in captivity, most remain in India. A pair in the Bristol Zoo in England has produced four young; a female is owned by the Crandon Park Zoo in Miami. Mohini and her offspring complete the list of those living elsewhere.

Because the fat and protein content of nursing milk varies widely among the big cats, Ted had searched all available zoo literature for information on tiger's milk. He found nothing. We settled on a commercial formula for baby animals, and Rewati took an ounce of it. Well, the first hurdle was behind us; we would vary the formula cautiously, guided by the cub's growth rate and bowel movements.

My youngest child is 18, so I had forgotten how exhausting a new baby in the house can be. When Rewati began yowling her first night, Ted and I awoke with a start. Two pairs of bare feet hit the floor in unison. Arriving simultaneously, side by side, at the nursery doorway, we managed to wedge through— the way millions of other parents have done. Rewati just wanted her bottle and a dry blanket.

From that time on, she wanted those bottles every 3½ hours around the clock. Soon, she would outgrow the incubator, graduate to an open box 2½ by 4 feet, and then move on to a larger pen in the basement.

On the tenth day of her life—two days after she arrived at the house—both her blue eyes were open. On the 13th day she managed a wobbly walk. On the 22nd day she exhibited signs of playfulness, shaking her towel like a puppy.

But her 24th day was the one I had been waiting for. Rewati slept the whole night through. And so did I.

Our first crisis came a few days later when we found the cub crawling in tight circles, unable to use her hind legs. My husband consulted the zoo's veterinarian and other specialists. They treated Rewati without being sure what her ailment was. Rewati received antibiotics, oxygen treatments, outside exercise sessions, and a formula bolstered with egg and brandy. In a week she was well again, roaming our newly fenced backyard, which had now become her "jungle."

Her weight had tripled by then, and she had begun to feed from a bowl—baby cereal and strained beef mixed in milk. Frankly, Rewati was a messy eater: I faced a cleanup project after every meal.

A tigress grooms her cubs by licking them. I used a damp washrag on Rewati, and she'd roll her ice-blue eyes blissfully during the ceremony.

There was nothing catlike about the way she walked: her lunging, rolling gait, in fact, reminded me more of a puppy. She would prowl the dim recesses behind the shrubs, pausing now and then to sharpen her claws on my camellia bushes, then pounce out to attack the big red plastic ball that was her favorite toy.

One member of our family viewed Rewati's arrival with something less than enthusiasm—Ebony, our big black tomcat. In those early days, he'd stand in the nursery doorway glaring balefully while I attended to the tiny cub. Or was it a hungry glare? I kept the two apart.

But as the white cub grew, Ebony's attitude changed to one of aloofness. Rewati wanted to be friendly. She even sidled up to the cat and gave him a playful nuzzle. Ebony leaped up on the fence and sat there outraged, licking furiously at the spot where he had been "contaminated."

Until the tiger arrived, Ebony had taken our affection for granted. Now he felt that his place in the Reed household was threatened. At the slightest provocation, the tomcat would leap up on my lap, doing his best to play the role of a cuddly kitten.

Suddenly Ebony's troubles doubled. The zoo bought an orange Bengal cub as a playmate for Rewati. She was Sakhi—in Hindi, "close and dear companion."

The white cub and the orange one would romp in the yard together, much to Ebony's disgust. It was amusing to watch the tomcat prepare to traverse tiger country. He'd plot his course across the yard carefully—and I'm sure he had escape routes in mind every foot of the way.

Rewati hated to be alone. As long as someone was within sight when she was in the yard—even Ebony—she was content. If she was left alone, I could count on hearing yowls and a scratching on my kitchen door. "Spoiled tiger," appeared more than once in the record I kept on our tenant.

I tended to forget, sometimes, that everyone does not have a tiger in his house. One day a man from the electric company came by to read the meter. Preoccupied, I waved him toward the basement where Rewati was napping. The meterman survived the shock—though I did get a polite phone call from the electric company asking how long I planned to keep that tiger down there.

Like all proud parents, we invited friends to "come see the baby," and they came by the dozens. I counted 35 adults and children in a single day. Ted brought fellow zoo officials home, too. He took one in to tiger-watch at midnight, and the stillness soon was shattered by tiger yowls. "Ted should let sleeping tigers lie" was my rather testy journal entry next day.

Sometimes, when Ted worked late, Rewati and I would watch television. The programs seemed a bit tame, though—with a white tiger curled up next to me on the couch.

She was my "$10,000 tiger." I managed to get used to that. Then Ted mentioned casually that she really was worth about $35,000 by now! I wished he hadn't told me.

I rarely left the house. But when it was absolutely necessary to go out, I'd round up a tiger-sitting friend and give her only one rule to follow. "If the house catches fire, just take the cub and leave."

By the 60th day, Rewati's weight had climbed to 15 pounds and she was now eating ground meat. Even in play, her teeth and claws could hurt.

Before, it had been easy to get tiger-sitters when I had to leave the house for a few hours; now there was less enthusiasm.

The time had come to send Rewati to her permanent home in the zoo where Bert Barker, head keeper of the large carnivores, could assume the mother's role. Sakhi—three weeks younger than her white playmate—would stay on in the house for a couple of weeks until she was on a solid food diet. Then she too would become a zoo resident.

The two cubs had a final romp in our yard that last day. Even Ebony sensed something, for his icy reserve melted a bit. Crossing the yard, he stopped to eye a waving tiger tail. He couldn't resist; for a few seconds he batted the tail back and forth with his paws. Then, recovering his dignity, Ebony stalked off.

Rewati went home to the zoo, and two weeks later Sakhi left. My house has never seemed so large and quiet.

Do I miss my tigers? There were times—especially during those 3 a.m. feedings—when I'd mutter, "May this house be safe from tigers." But miss them? Of course I do.

It is comforting, though, to remember that both Rewati and Sakhi are secure and healthy under the tender care of Bert Barker. And neither of them will ever be lonely, for hundreds of thousands of adults and children visiting the zoo enjoy my tigers now.

And there's always this: One day my phone is sure to ring again, and Ted will be at the other end of the line, saying "Get the nursery ready."

I wonder what kind of infant I'll be asked to mother then?

from NATIONAL GEOGRAPHIC

We Love You, Boris

HESTER MUNDIS

When I first saw Boris, he was lying on a blanket of shredded newspaper in a kitten carrying case in a not-so-reputable New York pet shop—a helpless, frightened, and unbelievably adorable orphan baby chimpanzee. Dark chocolate eyes were set in a light mocha face that was as soft as doeskin, and on his chin was a powder-white fuzz of a beard. His hair was silky and black and parted in the center of his head, bristling out at the sides around two outrageously comic big ears. Something this cute, I thought, could not be real. It was undoubtedly a very ingenious battery-operated toy. Somewhere on his underside there had to be a tag that said, "Made in Japan." But suddenly I was holding him, and there was no tag in sight. In one magic moment, he threw his arms around my neck, thoroughly wet my coat, and, though I did not know it then, totally annihilated a lifetime of rationality and logic.

Common sense didn't enter the picture. He needed a mom. I was already a working mother with an eight-year-old son and couldn't see what difference a chimp would make in our lives—and neither did my husband, Jerry. Boy, did we have a lot to learn! Boris changed all our lives completely and forever.

We raised him in our Manhattan apartment, along with our rambunctious German shepherd, Ahab, for nearly three years, learning the hard though often hilarious way that what is okay behavior in the jungle can be a disaster in an apartment—especially where the closest things to vines are drapes, pole lamps look like trees, and your prime playmate is the most-feared dog in the neighborhood. (Boris's early years were an expensive proposition, too. Aside from the 750 pounds of bananas he ate annually, antique vases that had come through the Revolution unscathed didn't survive 15 minutes with Boris.) But it wasn't until I discovered that I was expecting another baby that we realized Boris needed—and deserved—a permanent home of his own, with his own.

We researched all the zoos in the world (literally), and Chester Zoo in England was like an answer to our prayers. Not only had numerous animal authorities lauded it for its excellence, especially in its treatment of apes (who could romp and play on an island without bars), but the zoo's founder, Mr. Mottershead, assured us that Boris would never be given away for research and would have a home at Chester for life.

Boris knew something was amiss, and in the weeks and days before his departure he repeatedly tried to bring things back to normal, which scored us all the more. Whenever one of us would pet him lovingly, wistfully, in that poignantly brave but transparently sad way indicative of goodbyes, he would pull away and try to strike up a game or a chase. Sometimes he'd crawl up on my lap and roll over on his back, begging to be tickled. I'd force myself to giggle and laugh with him as I had in the past, but it fooled neither of us. I found myself encouraging him and Ahab in relay games. At least Ahab could play with him for extended periods without crying.

We made arrangements with BOAC (the British Overseas Airlines Corporation) to fly Boris to Manchester and bought a small, sturdy carrying case to ship him in. Although tranquilizers are often given to animals being shipped by air, we were advised against it. We changed Boris's flight to one that coincided with his bedtime and confirmed with Chester that someone from the zoo would be at the airport to meet him the following morning.

The day of Boris's departure arrived, as we'd known it would. I dressed him in his red and white polo shirt. He was excited and happy knowing that he was going out, which only tore more at my heart. The cab ride to Kennedy Airport was excruciatingly painful. Boris was loving every minute of peering out the window, and the taxi driver kept asking us why we were crying. It hurt too much to explain.

At the terminal, we prepared Boris's carrying case for the flight. We took a newspaper and shredded it, just as we had when we first brought him home from the pet store. We put it in the case along with some lettuce, apple slices, and a piece of my sweatshirt, which he'd always cuddled at night as a sort of security blanket. Then I undressed him and put him inside. Jerry grabbed my hand, and we kissed Boris goodbye. I couldn't stop the tears.

The next morning, we received a cable from the zoo telling us that Boris had arrived "safe, happy, and neatly packed." A week later we got a long, newsy letter from Mr. Mottershead telling us that Boris not only was doing well but was a hit with all the visitors, cutting up with antics and reveling in his increased audiences.

Photographs followed, and we were pleased to see that Boris's new friends looked like just the sort we wanted him to hang out with. As heart-wrenching a decision as it was to part with our little fluff ball, as we called him, he is happy at Chester.

In the 27 years that he has been there, Boris has thrived with the companionship of his own kind (he is now the proud father of 12) and basked in the attentive care of his keepers (one of whom, Neil Ormond, has been there since the day he arrived). Somehow, in his own special way, he's managed to bridge the evolutionary gap that separates men from apes— enjoying the rest of his days in the best of all alien worlds.

I visited him twice in the first 12 years he was there, each time bringing him his favorite foods (tiny marshmallows, raisins, and a chocolate Yoo-Hoo drink). He'd hoot, I'd cry, and partings were always difficult. It was May when I made my third visit; it had been 15 years since last I saw him.

Boris looked handsomer than ever! I realized that 15 years was a long time between visits and a lot had happened in both our lives, so once again I'd brought his favorite raisins and marshmallows to spark memories that could help him remember our connection.

At first it looked as if his only interest was in the food. But as I called out to him, using phrases he once knew, such as "What do you think of that?" and "Give me a kiss!" his attention became more focused on me. He hooted several times. I used to know what every one of his grunts and hoots meant when he was a baby, but this time I wasn't sure. (Indeed his voice had grown a lot deeper.) But when he went inside the chimp house, he stared at me through the glass.

For a long moment, we held each other with our eyes— mine, of course, filling with tears—and in his gaze there was a glint of recognition, a perception of something special between us. He might not have remembered me as his "mom," but he remembered something—and that meant everything to me. As we were walking away, I turned for one last look back.

Now, I might have imagined it—or it might have been the tears in my eyes—but his arm was outstretched, and I could have sworn he blew me a kiss goodbye.

Today Boris is the dominant chimp at the Chester Zoo and a favorite with visitors. His likeness appears on souvenir chocolate coins sold at the gift shop, which makes me smile. For me, he's always been what sweet dreams were made of.

from HEART SONGS FOR ANIMAL LOVERS

ACKNOWLEDGMENTS
(continued from page ii)

"The Pigeon Race" and "Little Warhorse, the History of a Jack-rabbit" are from *Animal Heroes,* by Ernest Thompson Seton. Copyright © 1987 by Creative Arts Book Company. Originally published by Charles Scribner's Sons in 1905.

"Watching the Loons" is from *The Wild Within,* by Paul Rezendes. Copyright © 1998 by Paul Rezendes. Published by Penguin Putnam Inc.

"Winged Spirit," by Jeanne B. Fletcher, and "We Love You, Boris," by Hester Mundis, are from *Heart Songs for Animal Lovers,* collected by Hester Mundis. Copyright © 1999 by Hester Mundis. Published by Rodale Books.

"A Bell for Rajah," by John K. Terres, is from *The Audubon Wildlife Treasury,* edited by Les Line. Copyright © 1976 by Les Line and the National Audubon Society. Published by J. B. Lippincott Company.

"The Newborn Whale" is from *The Mother Whale,* by Edith Thacher Hurd. Copyright © 1973 by Edith Thacher Hurd. Published by Little, Brown and Company.

"A Secret Place" and "Grubs and Petunia" are from *Secrets of a Wildlife Watcher,* by Jim Arnosky. Copyright © 1983 by Jim Arnosky. Published by Lothrop, Lee & Shepard Books.

"A Shark in Trouble" is from *Sevengill,* by Don C. Reed. Copyright © 1986 by Don C. Reed. Published by Alfred A. Knopf, Inc.

"Help for Henry" is from *The Vanishing Manatee,* by Margaret Goff Clark. Copyright © 1990 by Margaret Goff Clark. Published by Dutton Children's Books, a division of Penguin Books USA Inc.

"Saving Corky" is from *The True Story of Corky, the Blind Seal,* by Georgeanne Irvine. Copyright © 1987 by Georgeanne Irvine. Published by Scholastic Inc.

"The Alley Behind Our House," by Nathan Zimelman, is from *Ranger Rick,* July 1999. Published by the National Wildlife Federation.

"The Fox" is from *The Darkness Is Light Enough,* by Chris Ferris. Copyright © 1986 by Chris Ferris. Published by Penguin Books Ltd.

"The Invader" is from *A Ferret in the Vestry,* by Carol Hathorne. Copyright by Carol Hathorne 1995. Published by Monarch Publications.

"Sasha's Story," by Amanda J. Luke, is from *Cat Fancy,* July 1999.

"Montana Mike," by Lynn Donaldson, is from *People* magazine, June 1999.

"One of God's Creatures," by King Mswati III, Kingdom of Swaziland, is from *All the King's Animals,* by Cristina Kessler. Copyright © 1995 by Cristina Kessler. Published by Boyds Mill Press, Inc.

"The Cinderella Dog" is from *Gorillas in the Mist,* by Dian Fossey. Copyright © 1983 by Dian Fossey. Published by Houghton Mifflin Company.

"Valuable Lives" is from *All Wild Creatures Welcome,* by Patricia Curtis. Copyright © 1985 by Patricia Curtis. Published by E. P. Dutton.

"Where the Wild Things Are" is from a *Reader's Digest* condensation of *Animal ER,* by Tufts University School of Veterinary Medicine with Vicki Croke. Published by Penguin Putnam Inc.

"The Bears of Summer" is from a *Reader's Digest* condensation of *Summers With the Bears,* by Jack Becklund. Copyright © 1999 by Jack Becklund. Published by Hyperion.

"A Walk With My Friends" is from *Through a Window,* by Jane Goodall. Copyright © 1990 by Soko Publications Limited. Published by Houghton Mifflin Company.

"White Tiger in My House," by Elizabeth C. Reed, is from *National Geographic,* April 1970.

A Note From the Editors

$\mathcal{T}$ his original Guideposts series was created by the Book and Inspirational Media Division of the company that publishes *Guideposts,* a monthly magazine filled with true stories of people's adventures in faith. *Guideposts* is available by subscription. All you have to do is write to Guideposts, 39 Seminary Hill Road, Carmel, New York 10512. When you subscribe, each month you can count on receiving exciting new evidence of God's presence, His guidance and His limitless love for all of us.

Guideposts is also available on the Internet by accessing our home page on the World Wide Web at www.guideposts.org. Send prayer requests to our Monday morning Prayer Fellowship. Read stories from recent issues of our magazines, *Guideposts, Angels on Earth, Clarity, Guideposts for Kids* and *Guideposts for Teens,* and follow our popular book of daily devotionals, *Daily Guideposts.* Excerpts from some of our best-selling books are also available.